# PC Maintenan

*Dedication*

*To Audrey, Darren and Kirsty*

# PC Maintenance
## An Introduction to Upgrade and Repair

## Colin Grimston

A member of the Hodder Headline Group
LONDON • SYDNEY • AUCKLAND

First published in Great Britain 1997 by Arnold,
a member of the Hodder Headline Group,
338 Euston Road, London NW1 3BH

Whilst the advice and information in this book is believed to be true and
accurate at the date of going to press, neither the author nor the publisher
can accept any legal responsibility or liability for any errors or omissions
that may be made.

Trademarks:
All products, names and services that are known to be trademarks or service
marks have been appropriately capitalized. Neither the author nor the publisher
can attest to the accuracy of this information. Use of such a term does not affect
the validity of any trademark or service mark.

Warning:
Every care has been taken with the production of this book to ensure that any
program, modification, projects, etc. described operate in a correct and safe manner.
However, neither the author nor the publisher or its dealers and distributors shall
be liable with respect to any liability, loss or damage caused or alleged to be
caused directly or indirectly by this book. Please note also that if equipment
that is still under warranty is modified in any way or connected to home-built
equipment, then that warranty may become void.

*British Library Cataloguing in Publication Data*
A catalogue record for this book is available from the British Library

ISBN 0 340 64545 8

Produced and typeset in 11/13 pt GaramondITC by Gray Publishing, Tunbridge Wells, Kent
Printed and bound in Great Britain by J. W. Arrowsmith Ltd, Bristol

# Contents

# *Preface*

Have you ever picked up one of those big impressive books about computers – the ones that you take to the local pub to impress your friends, but can't understand past page 5? Do you wish that you had a book that explained the basic terms in a language as simple as possible, but still gave you some idea about such things as Pentiums, plug and play, and burst mode operation? If your answer to both questions is **yes** then I could have the answer for you.

*PC Maintenance – An Introduction to Upgrade and Repair*, as the name suggests is an introduction to the world of personal computers. An introduction it might be, but it still provides the reader with up-to-date information on current developments.

The book is divided into four parts. The first consists of Chapters 1–6 which aim to build a foundation of knowledge about the hardware used, the expansion facilities and system configuration. Chapters 7 and 8 make up the next two parts: the first introduces the concept of fault finding on the PC and offers guidance in the form of troubleshooting flowcharts, and the second offers a selection of exercises and upgrading guides to help you put your new-found knowledge into practice. The final part consists of a series of appendices supporting your knowledge with technical information and system record forms.

Chapter 1 provides brief details about the development of the PC over the last decade, concentrating mainly on the AT version since the introduction of the 80286.

Chapter 2 takes you 'inside the box' and explains the basic features of the power supply unit, the system board including microprocessor, memory and support chips, disk drives, and CD-ROM drives. Throughout this chapter I have attempted to keep the terminology and explanations simple in such a way that by the end you will be able to formulate your own understanding of system operations. An understanding of this chapter will help in later discussions.

Chapter 3 walks you through developments in microprocessor technology gradually building on block diagrams from the basic processor to discuss eventually the latest technology for the Pentium, Pentium Pro and Nx686.

Chapter 4 helps you to catch the bus – the expansion bus! The PC would not be what it is today if it were not for the flexibility offered with adaptor slots. This chapter will certainly help you to sort out your ISA from your VESA, and even look at MCA, PCI and PCMCIA.

Chapter 5 looks at the teminology and developments associated with memory. You will not be bored with long discussions of early memory devices; the chapter focuses on SIMMs, their application and arrangements.

Chapter 6 is essential reading for the PC user. It introduces you to the set-up facilities that are used to configure your system, and looks at the problems arising from IRQs.

Chapter 7 helps to develop your understanding and introduces you to diagnostic tools and utilities. The chapter provides a set of user-friendly flowcharts that are intended to help you to develop the right troubleshooting approach.

Chapter 8 shows you how to take a PC to pieces and put it back together again. The practical exercises provide the basic methods used, and the upgrading guides build on this experience, taking you through the basic steps for installing disk drives, CD-ROM drives, sound cards and memory.

Finally, the appendices provide essential forms for recording your system details, technical information to help you to identify the different cards and connectors, and a list of typical error codes generated by a PC's own self-test program. The information provided is mainly for use with the practical exercises and is intended to bring some sort of realism to the text.

There is a wealth of information describing the ancient history of the PC, from the early days of the Altair 8080, considered the first PC, to the present high-powered Pentium-based machines. Since the primary purpose of this book is of a practical nature, aimed at providing the reader with an underpinning knowledge to support practical skills in the assembley, upgrade and repair of common PCs, the text will be concise and to the point, omitting much of the unnecessary jargon and debate to be found in many books.

## Basic jargon

In any technical subject it is all to easy for the knowledgeable person to use terminology and jargon which to the beginner sound impossible. You are reminded that the glossary provides the reader with an explanation of many of the terms necessary for a basic understanding of the subject, but it makes sense to include in each chapter a summary of the common terms for newcomers to the subject. Any new terms introduced in a chapter are highlighted in *italics*, and an explanation included under the heading 'Basic jargon'.

## Acknowledgement

The author wishes to thank Michael Boyle for preparing the artworks.

# 1
# What is a PC?

## A PC is . . .

As with so many of life's modern machines the personal computer is often easily recognizable, but is difficult to define, and to a great extent the term has been superseded by developments in technology. By definition the PC is designed for use by an individual, rather than a group of people, and characteristically tends to be an interactive, affordable computer with its origins derived from the original IBM Personal Computer.

Although once the cover is removed no two PCs could be considered identical, the external appearance of different makes and models can be very similar. These external similarities are mainly functional in the sense that there are a few basic needs of the user which have to be considered. Any computer system needs to be provided with facilities for entering data and commands, giving details of what the computer is doing, storage of data, and somewhere to house the electronic bits and pieces.

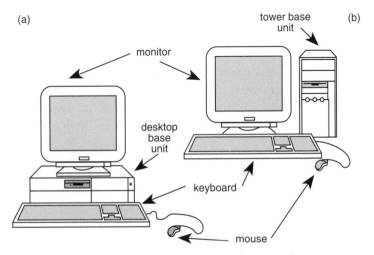

**Figure 1.1** (a) Typical desktop system; (b) typical tower system

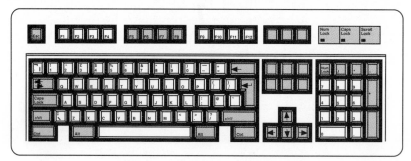

**Fig. 1.2**  A modern AT keyboard

There are four basic units recognizable to the user: the system base unit (the box), monitor, keyboard, and mouse. Although these units may come in a variety of shapes and sizes, the purpose of each remains principally the same. These basic units can be identified from the diagrams in Fig. 1.1, which show typical *desktop* and tower systems.

❏ The system base unit is a metal box, housing all of the main functional parts of the PC, i.e. the electronic circuitry, power supply, *memory*, and disk drives.
❏ The monitor provides a visual display that gives feedback on what the computer is doing, and on data and commands entered by the user. In appearance the monitor looks very much like a portable television.
❏ The keyboard enables the user to enter data and commands into the system. The standard PC keyboard is based on the typewriter QWERTY layout, but has several more dedicated keys helping to provide a flexible system. The modern enhanced Advanced Technology (AT) keyboard, shown in Fig. 1.2, has 102 keys in total, compared to the original Extended Technology (XT) which had only 84 keys.

The monitor and keyboard are the main components enabling communication with the system, but the mouse is essential for use as a pointing device with many of today's applications.

❏ The mouse is a small plastic box connected to the system base unit via a thin cable, providing an additional input device. Although most functions can be performed without the aid of a mouse, the use of applications is much simplified and faster using the mouse as a pointing device.

## The PC and XT

Before looking in any depth at the technical developments of the PC, it is interesting to consider first the early decisions made in the computer industry that led to the introduction of the IBM PC. The computer was originally conceived as an electronic curiosity aimed at the hobbyist already exploring programming with other computers. Early success in this market and increased awareness by business users were the incentives for further development that led to the IBM Desktop *PC*.

Announced by IBM in 1981, the original PC housed an 8 *bit*, 8088 *microprocessor*, and supported the following:

❏ 64 Kb of *RAM*
❏ 2 × 360 Kb floppy disk (*diskette*) drives
❏ an 80 column × 25 line *text display*
❏ up to 16 colours using a *colour graphics adaptor* (*CGA*)
❏ RAM upgradable to 640 *Kilobytes (Kb)*.

It was in 1982 that saw the emergence of the XT version of the PC. Initially, this provided the user with a single floppy disk drive with additional *hard disk drive* facility. The standard configuration soon became a computer with a hard disk drive and two floppy drives.

**Table 1.1**  Summary of main system developments

| System base | Date of introduction | Micro-procesor | Typical RAM | Floppy disk | Hard disk | Graphics | Maximum speed |
|---|---|---|---|---|---|---|---|
| PC | 1981 | 8088 | 256 Kb | 360 Kb | None | Text/CGA | 8 *MHz* |
| XT | 1982 | 8088 80286 | 640 Kb 720 Kb | 360 Kb | 10 *Mb* | Text/CGA | 10 MHz |
| AT | 1984 | 80286 | 1 Mb | 1.2 Mb 720 Kb | 20 Mb | Text/CGA or EGA | 16 MHz |
| 386DX | 1986 | '386DX | 2 Mb | 1.2 Mb 1.44 Mb | 100 Mb | Text,VGA or *SVGA* | 40 MHz |
| 386SX | 1988 | '386SX | 2 Mb | 1.44 Mb 1.2 Mb | 100 Mb | Text,VGA or SVGA | 40 MHz |
| 486DX | 1990 | '486DX | 4 Mb | 1.2 Mb 1.44 Mb | 340 Mb | VGA or SVGA | 33–40 MHz |
| 486SX | 1991 | '486SX | 4 Mb | 1.2 Mb 1.44 Mb | 340Mb | VGA or SVGA | 33 MHz |
| 486DX2 | 1992 | '486DX2 | 8 Mb | 1.44 Mb | 540 Mb | SVGA | 50 and 66 MHz |
| 486DX4 | 1994 | '486DX4 | 8 Mb | 1.44 Mb | 850 Mb | SVGA | 100 MHz |
| Pentium | 1993 | Pentium | 16 Mb | 1.44 Mb | To 1 Gb | SVGA | 75–166 MHz |

Compact disk–read only memory (*CD-ROM*) drives have increased in popularity since around 1994, and are commonly used in '486 systems onwards. Recent months have seen a substantial increase in availability at realistic cost with ×8 speed CD-ROMs currently being standard.

Much has been written about these developments, and although these early machines were based on the 8088 microprocessor, there was available at the time a microprocessor superior to the 8088, that is the 8086. As the numbering system suggests, the 8086 was first to be produced, but it was not used extensively owing to the poor availability of inexpensive support components. Modern microprocessors and their numbering systems are derived from the 8086.

Continued developments resulted in the production of an AT version, with considerable improvements on the earlier PC and XT. The earlier PC/XT systems will not be discussed further, owing to their rapid advancement into the realms of ancient technology.

## The AT

The AT computer announced by IBM in 1984 used a new, faster processor, the 80286. As with the 8086, this was designed to handle 16 bits of data and operate at much higher speeds, but was not constrained in its use by the availability of support components. The standard system remained as a combination of hard and floppy disk drives. Continued development of the PC was, and still is, based on two main factors – further improvements in the microprocessor, and increased capacity of both memory and disk drives.

Table 1.1 provides a summary of the main factors associated with the development of the PC. The facts and figures quoted are generally accepted to be those typical of systems at the peak of their popularity. Any specialist developments from an individual manufacturer have not been included.

## Summary

The past decade has seen major changes in the world of computers. The PC is no exception, with a product developing from a fairly basic PC or XT to the modern powerful Pentium systems. Memory of at least 8 Mb, hard disk drives with capacities over 1 Gb (1024 Mb), microprocessor speeds in excess of 160 MHz, and high-*resolution* displays make the modern PC a formidable machine.

## Basic jargon

*Bit.* Used to describe a binary digit. It is the smallest unit of data in a digital system, having one of two values, 1 (on), or 0 (off). The term 'bit' will not be shortened when used as a unit of measurement.

*Byte.* A standard measure of memory and disk size, the byte consists of 8 bits of data. When used as a unit of measurement the term byte will be abbreviated to the lower-case letter 'b'.

*CD-ROM.* CD–read only memory. An optical storage medium similar to the audio compact disk (CD), used for permanent storage of data and programs. Although the information on an original pressing cannot be changed, it is now possible to obtain specialist equipment that enables the user to write to a CD-ROM.

*CGA display.* The colour graphics adaptor introduced colour to the world of PCs, allowing simple graphics as well as text.

*CMOS.* Complementary metal oxide semiconductor – refers to a popular method of chip construction.

*Desktop PC.* For the purposes of this book the desktop PC will be considered to be that shown in Fig. 1.1(a) based on the original IBM AT design.

*Diskette.* A magnetically coated disk used for the storage of data or programs. Also called a floppy disk, the diskette can be removed from the disk drive.

*Hard disk drive.* A magnetic storage medium similar in purpose to the diskette, but with much greater capacity, and of a sealed-drive unit construction. The hard disk drive is not normally removable from the PC, but is designed as such in modern notebook and laptop systems.

*Kilobyte.* Equivalent to 1024 bytes (8192 bits). The term Kilo should not be confused with the traditional meaning. In everyday use, kilo (k) refers to a multiple of 1000, but in computer terms the value for kilo (K) is 1024, e.g. 1 Kb = 1024 b = 8192 bits.

*Megabyte.* Equivalent to 1024 kilobytes (1 048 576 bytes or 8 388 608 bits). In everyday use, mega refers to a multiple of 1 000 000, but in computer terms the value is 1 048 576, e.g. 1 Mb = 1024 Kb = 1 048 576 b = 8 388 608 bits.
    In real terms, 1 Mb can be approximated to the amount of space in memory, or on disk, that is needed to store about 1 000 000 characters.

*Megahertz (MHz).* Hertz is a unit of measurement of frequency (the number of times a signal changes per second). Megahertz represents a million changes per second.

*Memory.* An area consisting of electronic chips used to store data and instructions. Capacity is measured in bytes, Kb or Mb.

*Microprocessor.* Often thought of as the 'brains' of a computer, the microprocessor temporarily stores and executes program instructions on data.

*RAM.* Random access memory. A specific type of memory used for temporary storage of data or instructions. It is continually written to and read from while the computer is operating.

*Resolution.* A term used in video to describe the number of pixels, or dots, that can be displayed on a monitor screen. A high resolution results in a well-defined, clear image.

*ROM.* Read only memory. A specific type of memory that under normal operation may be considered as permanent, i.e. cannot be altered by the user.

*SVGA display.* The super virtual graphics array extends the number of modes used with standard VGA, providing even greater resolution.

*System speed*. A measure of the speed or frequency of the system clock that keeps the whole system in time. Sometimes referred to as clock speed, it is measured in MHz.

*Text display*. The original text displays used with monitors enabled text to be displayed on a different coloured background. Any form of graphics was text based and of poor quality.

*VGA display*. The virtual graphics array forms the basis of standards used today. It allows the use of 256 colours and offers much improved resolution, producing good-quality graphics.

# 2
# Inside the box

## The cover removed

Once 'inside the box', the user is either mystified or horrified. Whichever group you fall into, there is nothing to fear, so long as you have a basic understanding of what is happening and are careful to observe essential precautions. The basis for those precautions are listed below, and are discussed in more detail in Chapter 7.

- Have a large clear space to work on.
- Take great care that foreign objects do not fall into the case.
- Pay particular attention to the safety notes provided in Appendix A and in later chapters.
- Although there are times when it may be necessary to operate the system with the cover removed, you are advised to keep this practice to a minimum, certainly until you are familiar with the system and its operation.
- There are specific precautions relating to static electricity. It is not essential at this point to understand in detail the issues surrounding static discharge, but you should always take antistatic precautions when touching components inside the case.

One helpful advantage of working on PCs, compared to working on other electronic equipment, is that there are similarities in the physical structure and layout of most makes and models. Construction is of a modular design in which the modules are often referred to as *field replaceable units* (*FRUs*), the most obvious modules within a system being the power supply, disk/compact disk–read only memory (CD-ROM) drives, *system board* and *adaptor cards*. Although the main text of this book will relate to a typical *desktop clone*, diagrams will be provided throughout to show similarities or differences between the desktop clone, tower, and typical *compatible* systems.

In the majority of systems, the basic structure of the base unit consists of a metal chassis to which several component modules are fastened. The metal

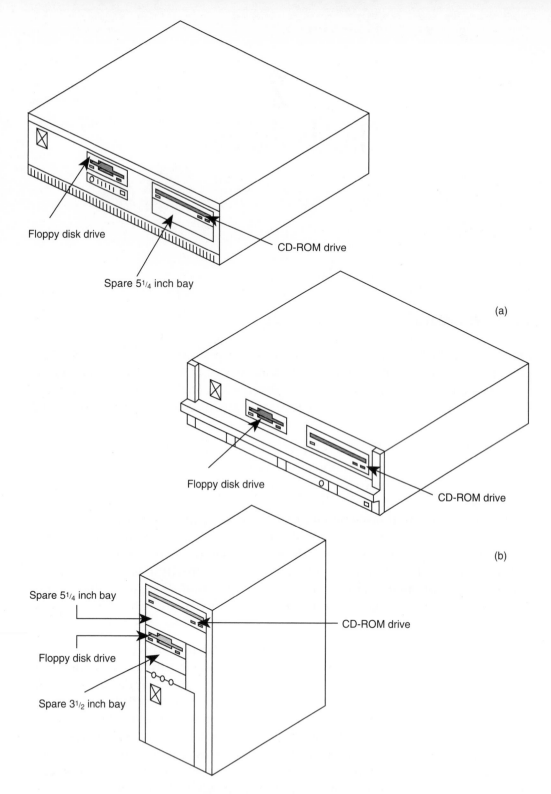

**Fig. 2.1** (a) Desktop system base unit; (b) compatible system base unit; (c) tower system base unit

chassis is constructed in two parts. The upper part forms the cover, or outer casing, which is mainly for protection, but also acts to reduce radiated interference with other electrical equipment. The lower part of the chassis forms a base to house the system board, the power supply, *drive bays* for the floppy and hard disk drives, CD-ROM drives, loudspeaker, switches, and mounting brackets. The construction of a range of system base units can be seen clearly in Fig. 2.1.

The front and back of the lower chassis are usually formed to provide front and rear panels. The rear panel provides the user with facilities for inter-connecting the base unit to other essential equipment. It has a mains supply socket, keyboard, monitor and mouse connections with sockets provided for peripherals such as printer, *modem*, and joystick. Rear panel layouts for desktop clone, compatible and tower systems are shown in Fig. 2.2. The most significant differences can be seen in the positions of the *port* sockets for the desktop and

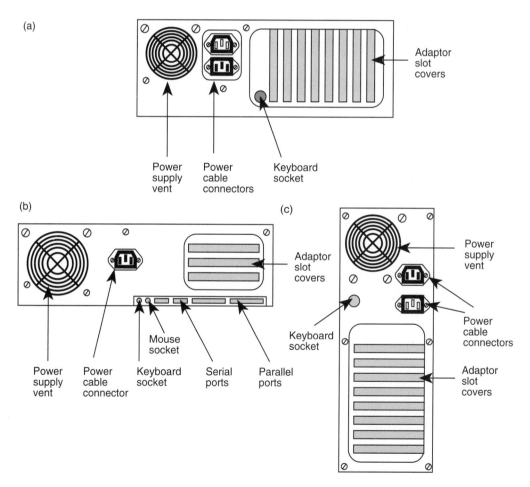

**Fig. 2.2**   Rear panel view of (a) desktop clone; (b) compatible; (c) tower

the compatible. As can be seen in Fig. 2.2(b) the sockets are placed along the base of the rear panel. This is because in the compatible base unit the expansion ports are contained on the system board rather than on *expansion cards*.

In many tower systems, the layout is basically that of a desktop, but turned on to its side.

The front panel of the chassis, illustrated in Fig. 2.3, provides the switch buttons for power, system speed, and reset, and also gives access to the floppy disk and CD-ROM drives. Figure 2.3 (a) and (b) show desktop systems, and (c) shows a typical tower system with the cover removed. Modern PCs also have a digital display that indicates to the user the selected operating speed of the system.

## Power supply unit

When fully assembled and operating, perhaps the most noticeable feature of the base unit is the whirring of the power supply, or to be more precise, the fan within the power supply unit (PSU).

The PSU houses many electronic components generating sufficient heat to require a forced cooling system. This is provided by a cooling fan mounted within the PSU case, which draws cooling air through the casing and forces warm air out of the vent on the rear panel shown in Figs 2.2 and 2.4. Most PCs also rely on the power supply fan to circulate air through the rest of the case. Airflow around expansion cards and the system board components is necessary to prevent a build-up of temperature, and hence to prolong the life of components.

It is essential that the airpath is not restricted, either through the fan vent on the rear panel, or through any cooling slots or holes. For this reason a system base unit must never be operated in confined places with inadequate air circulation, such as cupboards, or with the rear panel pushed up against a wall.

It should be noted that if the fan ever stops running you should switch off the system immediately to prevent overheating, and have the fault repaired.

The PSU is shown in Fig. 2.4. It consists of a metal case, approximately 210 mm × 140 mm × 120 mm high, which is mounted to the base chassis and rear panel, towards one corner.

The main functions of the power supply are:

- to convert 240 V *a.c.* from the mains supply into a lower *voltage* suitable for electronic components. In a computer there are two voltages produced from the power supply, 5 V and 12 V *d.c.* to power the component parts of the system. Output connecting leads are provided to the *system board* and the drives
- to provide some overload protection. This is in effect an electronic fuse which turns off the system if an electrical fault develops in the computer, the power supply, or the mains supply.

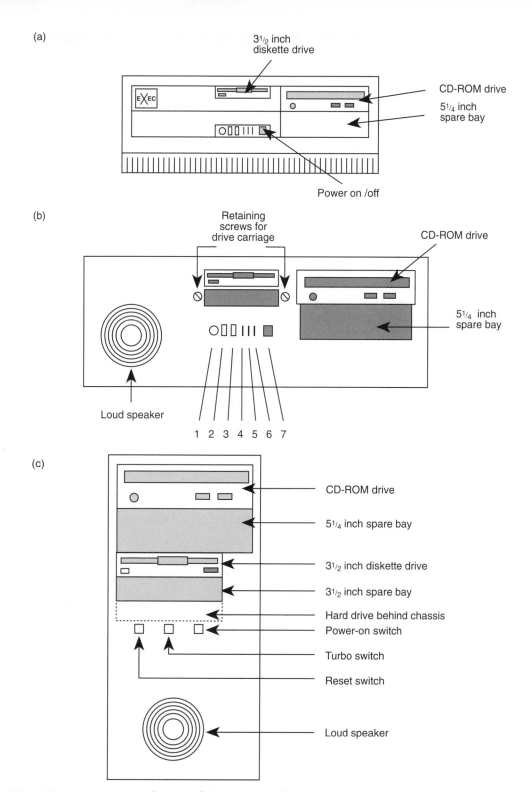

**Fig. 2.3** (a) Front panel view of desktop; (b) front panel view of desktop with cover removed: 1, keylock; 2, reset; 3, turbo; 4, hard drive LED; 5, turbo LED; 6, power LED; 7, power switch; (c) front panel view of tower with cover removed

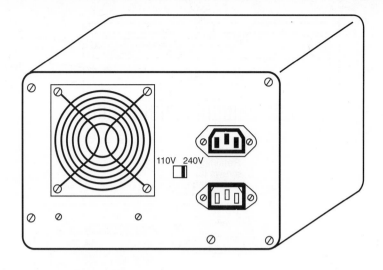

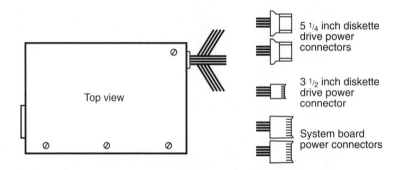

**Fig. 2.4**   Typical power supply

The *block diagram* in Fig. 2.5 shows the various stages in converting the 240 V mains supply into a lower working voltage needed for electronic components. The diagram is provided for interest only, it should be appreciated that the power supply is a very complicated piece of electronics, with potentially lethal voltages inside. For this very reason the following warning is given:

> **The cover of the power supply unit must never be removed except by a qualified electronics or electrical engineer**

The operating supply voltage varies from country to country. Many power supplies provide a switchable input selector for use on 240 V or 110 V, as shown in Fig. 2.4. Using a PC from a 240 V mains supply, when switched to 110 V, can result in serious damage, so it is important not to tamper with this selector.

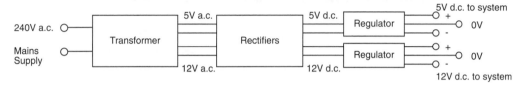

**Fig. 2.5**   Simplified diagram of a power supply unit

The power supply operation involves converting 240 V a.c. into 5 V d.c. and 12 V d.c. The process requires the voltage to be reduced, changed to d.c, and then controlled to prevent variation. A *transformer* is used to reduce the incoming supply voltage to a value slightly higher than the 5 V and 12 V needed. This is followed by several *rectifiers* that allow *current* to flow in one direction only, hence converting the now lower voltage from a.c. to d.c. Finally, the *regulator* is an electronic circuit that adjusts the voltage to a precise level, and prevents unwanted variations in the outputs. As can be seen from Fig. 2.5, the voltages needed by the PC's circuits are $+5$ V, $-5$ V, $+12$ V and $-12$ V, with several common 0 V.

The actual power supply used in a PC is a *switch mode power supply* and is much more complex than that described above. Having additional monitoring and feedback circuitry, the alternating voltage applied to the transformer is switched on and off several thousand times per second. It is the rate of switching that controls the d.c. output voltage.

*PSU TO SYSTEM BOARD CONNECTIONS*

A popular method of connecting the power supply outputs to the system board is by using two connecting plugs, each with six pins as shown in Fig. 2.6(a). Figure 2.6(b) illustrates a single 10-pin plug used in some older compatible machines.

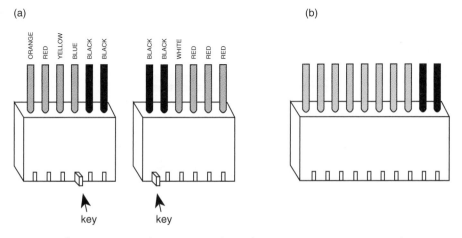

**Fig. 2.6**   Power supply to system board connectors: (a) six-pin; (b) 10-pin

**WARNING!**

These plugs must be connected correctly otherwise serious damage may result. In Fig. 2.7 the BLACK leads of each plug are shown adjacent to one another when connected to the system board; this is typical of the majority of systems.

When removing any connector, record carefully the method and polarity of each connection before removal. Consult your manual if in doubt.

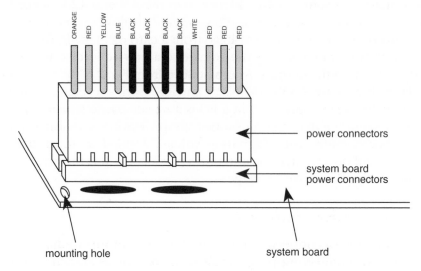

**Fig. 2.7**   Power supply leads connected to system board

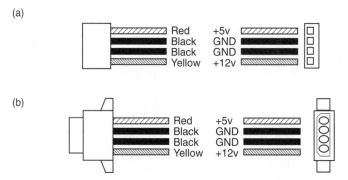

**Fig. 2.8**   Power supply connector for (a) floppy disk drive; (b) hard disk drive and older floppy disk drives

*PSU TO DRIVE CONNECTIONS*

The power supply also supplies the floppy/hard disk drives and the CD-ROM drives, using a single connector with four pins. There are two basic types as indicated in Fig. 2.8. The connector shown in Fig. 2.8(a) is the standard type used for floppy disk drives, and that in (b) is used for hard disk, CD-ROM, and some older floppy disk drives.

# System board (motherboard)

The most noticeable piece of electronic circuitry within the PC case is the system board, a circuit board covered with a wide range of different electronic components varying in size and function. The system board contains all of the basic electronics needed for the computer. The term 'basic' is used to indicate the essential requirements that are not usually categorized as 'add-ons', as distinct from basic meaning simple. In fact, the functional components of the system board could not be described, in any way or form, as simple.

The system board in a modern PC is much smaller than its counterpart of a few years ago. A modern board typically measures 332 mm × 218 mm (13 inches × 8.5 inches), but come as small as 165 mm × 218 mm (6.5 inches × 8.5 inches). The board is mounted using plastic stand-offs to the base of the chassis. These stand-offs are illustrated more clearly in Chapter 8 – Practical Exercises: System Disassembly, which discusses the correct procedures for removal of the system board from the base unit.

The layout of a typical system board is shown in Fig. 2.9 with a simplified block diagram of a complete system in Fig. 2.10. Each block in the block diagram represents a specific function, and may consist of one or more *integrated circuits*. The broad lines represent interconnections through which data, address information, or control signals are directed. These are commonly referred to individually as the *data, address* and *control bus,* respectively.

Many of the functions and terms outlined in the block diagram were associated with the original PC, and used individual *chips* for each. In the following notes, all functions and terms are described separately, but it must be remembered that currently a whole range of *chipsets* exists that combine many of the functions either into a single very large scale integration (*VLSI*) device, or within the processor itself.

*MICROPROCESSOR*

The underlying functions of a computer, to execute the instructions forming part of the program and to process associated data, are performed by the *central processing unit* (*CPU* or simply processor). In a PC many of the functions of the CPU are performed by a single processor chip – the *microprocessor*. In many IBM-compatible PCs the microprocessor chip will belong to, or be based on the

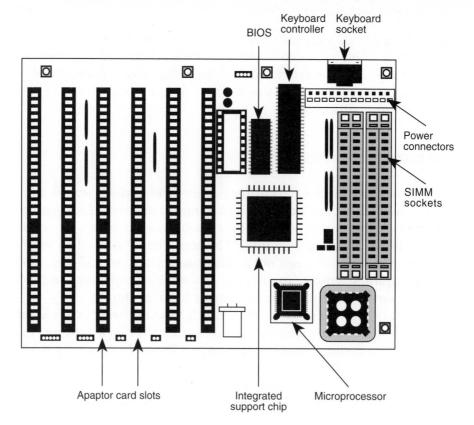

**Fig. 2.9**   Typical system board layout

Intel x86 family of processors. Although recognized as world leaders, Intel are not the only manufacturers of PC processors. Companies such as Cyrix, AMD and NexGen produce 'clone' processor chips that all run the same software, but perhaps with slightly different performance ratings.

It must be appreciated that this humble piece of silicon, the microprocessor, is a very complex device consisting of up to 3 100 000 transistors in the modern Pentium processor. To put this into the context of everyday life, if we assume that a single modern transistor would normally occupy an area 3 mm$^2$ on a traditional circuit board, the transistors in the Pentium would require an area of about 5.2 m$^2$.

*FLOATING POINT UNIT*

The floating point unit (FPU) is a coprocessor that can be thought of as an assistant processor. Effectively wired in parallel with the microprocessor, the FPU takes over some of the more complex tasks, thus freeing up the processor's time. It becomes active when instructions are processed relating to complex mathematics such as those with spreadsheet applications or computer-aided drawing.

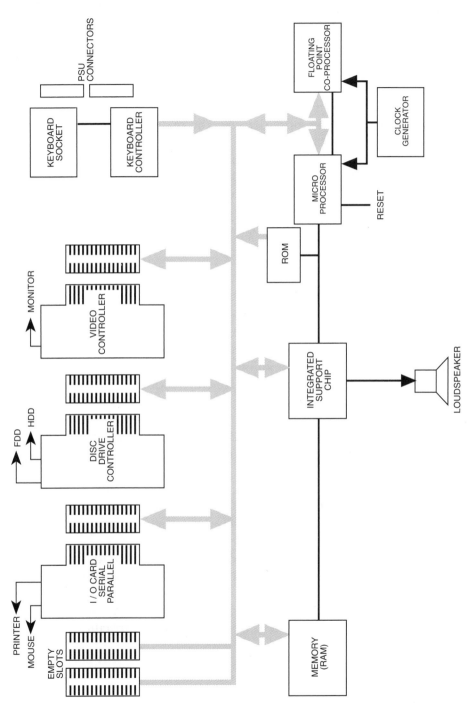

**Fig. 2.10** Simplified block diagram of system board

## MEMORY

The creation of a working computer is impossible without some form of memory. Memory is used generally to store programs, instructions to be processed by the microprocessor, and data that are created or to be used. The amount and type of memory in a system is dictated by the complexity of the program and number of instructions, together with the amount of data to be processed. Types of memory vary considerably, including the use of main memory, *cache* and *registers* for short-term storage, with even disk drives, CD-ROMs and *tape streamers* being considered as long-term memory devices. The main differences are associated with capacity, speed, and cost: the more you require in terms of greater capacity and faster access, the greater the cost. This introduces another important feature of both memory and storage devices, the maximum time taken to write to or read from a location. This time is referred to as the *access time*.

Even though memory continues to be developed and improved, there are two basic terms used that need to be recognized: random access memory (RAM) and read only memory (ROM).

## RANDOM ACCESS MEMORY (RAM)

RAM is a general term used to describe read–write memory devices used for temporary storage of data or instructions. This is volatile memory, which means that if power is removed, all data stored in the RAM are lost. Banks of RAM are used in PCs, depending on the amount of memory required, and are easily recognizable by the rows of identical small chips mounted either on the system board or on small circuit boards plugged into the system board.

CMOS RAM is a special type of RAM used for a specific purpose. It is used to store configuration data for the PC, and is maintained by the systems *CMOS set-up* utility. This usually includes information about numbers and types of floppy/hard disk drives, video adaptor, coprocessor, and amount of memory, plus the responsibility for holding the current date and time. Because the storage medium is volatile, it needs to be battery maintained using a small back-up battery, and is normally only modified when the system is new or has changed, or when the battery has deteriorated.

Cache memory uses very high speed RAM to compensate for bottlenecks resulting from the processor trying to access slower main memory RAM. It is particularly important for storing and accessing data used regularly by the microprocessor. Cache is becoming very popular on modern systems, with chips mounted on the system board providing capacities ranging from 32 to 1024 Kb.

## READ ONLY MEMORY

As the name implies read only memory (ROM) cannot be altered but only read. This type of memory is loaded into a chip once only, usually by the manufacturer, and used to store data that will not change. An example is that of the basic input/output system (BIOS), which contains software accessed when the system is switched on.

## BIOS

An operating system such as DOS does not communicate directly with your hardware, and as a result there needs to be a method of control until the point at which the operating system takes over. When initially powering up, the processor knows nothing about the system in which it is based, and cannot even access a disk drive. The BIOS programs control the system during this initialization process in preparation for use. One or more ROM chips which contain the BIOS are mounted on the system board.

The main functions of the BIOS are listed below:

- to test the system using the power-on self test (POST) when switched on. This tests the system board, memory, disk controllers, video controllers, keyboard and other main system components
- as a software interface providing access to all hardware components of the system
- to act as a 'bootstrap loader' which initiates a search for an operating system on the disk drives, loads the system into memory, and finally transfers control to the operating system.

ROMs can be identified as larger DIL chips with 24 or 28 pins, which are often in sockets making replacement simpler. Reasons for replacement do not have to be based on faults. Early BIOS versions sometimes had limitations, or were not compatible with later operating systems, making it necessary to upgrade to a later BIOS version. For example, an upgrade might be needed to support a new type of floppy disk drive not catered for by an older existing BIOS.

## EXPANSION (BUS) SLOTS

The PC provides the user with great flexibility by making the power, data, address, and control bus connections available on a number of *expansion slot* connectors. These connectors permit the use of adaptor cards, allowing the system to be configured to a variety of different monitors, drives and other peripheral devices. Figure 2.11 illustrates a typical adaptor card. The development of these expansion slots and associated cards has progressed on a par with the microprocessor, enabling fast interaction between the main system components and peripheral devices.

Each expansion slot provides:

- access for data, address and control buses to installed adaptors
- d.c. supply to power the adaptor cards and in some cases the additional devices.

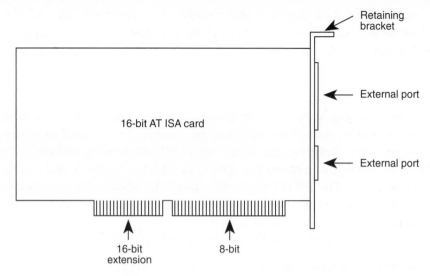

Retaining bracket

External port

16-bit AT ISA card

External port

16-bit extension

8-bit

**Fig. 2.11**   Typical adaptor card

*SYSTEM CLOCK/CLOCK GENERATOR*

A clock generator is an electronic circuit built into a chip, which provides regular timing signals for synchronizing and timing purposes. The clock generator used as the system clock in a PC synchronizes the entire system via the microprocessor, and produces '*ready*' and '*reset*' signals. Derived from a *crystal oscillator* the clock frequency is divided down to produce the clock signals for the various interface circuits.

   The clock can be thought of as keeping the system in check, and ticking at several million times per second, where one million times per second is referred to as one megahertz (1 MHz). The speed at which the clock runs is determined by the type and speed of the processor used. Hence a 486–33 MHz processor will use a clock speed of 33 MHz (33 million ticks per second). It is not advisable to run the processor at a higher speed than rated, not only because the processor may become 'confused', but also that a higher speed may result in the processor overheating. Although most modern computers no longer have a separate system clock chip, the associated crystal is easy to spot as a small metal can, stamped with a number representing the frequency of operation.

   The system clock should not be confused with the real time clock (RTC) which is derived from another source and is used in maintaining the time and date.

*KEYBOARD CONTROLLER*

The keyboard controller has two basic functions, to transmit and receive data from the keyboard, and to interrupt the microprocessor when data are ready for transfer. The chip consists of its own microprocessor with built-in ROM, RAM, clock generator and input/output ports.

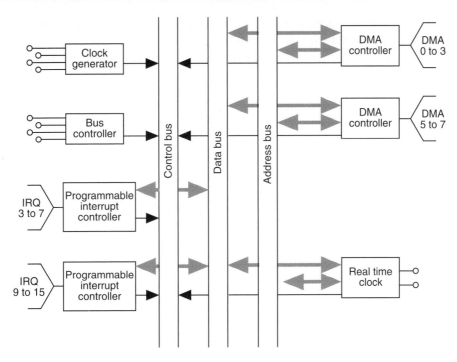

**Fig 2.12**   Integrated support chip

*INTEGRATED SUPPORT CHIP*

The chip count in modern PCs has been reduced significantly by integrating several of the functions associated with the original PC chips into a single device. These functions, originally undertaken by individual chips vary between manufacturers, but typically might include any of those described below. Consequently, the range of terms used to describe these integrated chips also varies.

A typical example would include the 80C206 integrated peripheral controller, which offers single chip integration and incorporates two DMA controllers, two interrupt controllers, one timer/counter, and one real-time clock, with other interfaces added for good measure. 80C206 is a typical manufacturer's identification number used in the same way that microprocessors are labelled 80486, etc.

Figure 2.12 outlines a block diagram showing the basic functions undertaken by a typical integrated support chip, and the following paragraphs provide a brief introduction to each.

*BUS CONTROLLER*

The control of the *system bus* can be delegated to special circuitry dedicated to the task, the bus controller. As the name implies, the bus controller has the task of controlling the flow of data and control signals across the buses. This is achieved by decoding outputs from the microprocessor to generate standard bus commands, and control signals to enable data on to buses, to determine direction of the flow of data, and to strobe addresses into the address latches.

## DMA CONTROLLER

Direct memory access (DMA) is a process that enables the transfer of data at high speed without the control of the microprocessor. It enables a device, such as a floppy or hard disk drive, to communicate directly with the system's main memory, instead of through the microprocessor. The DMA controller takes control over the system bus whilst the transfer takes place. Each device connected to the DMA system has a special channel assigned to enable identification.

This method of improving the speed of data flow has now been superseded by more efficient techniques such as *bus mastering*, but as you will learn in later chapters, these methods still need to use, and be assigned to, a DMA channel.

## PROGRAMMABLE INTERRUPT CONTROLLER

The programmable interrupt controller (PIC) continually monitors devices within the system, and sends an interrupt message to the processor if any device requires specific attention, e.g. pressing a key on the keyboard. A hardware interrupt signal generated by the device and managed by the PIC causes the processor to cease its current action and respond to the interrupting device. Once acknowledged, the processor then reads the data bus and takes appropriate action.

Requests from devices are evaluated and prioritized by the PIC with a high priority given to the keyboard, and a much lower priority to other devices such as the hard disk drive controller.

## PROGRAMMABLE INTERVAL TIMER/COUNTER

The microprocessor relies on the programmable interval timer (PIT) when timing and counting interrupt sequences. Often simply referred to as the timer/counter, the PIT contains typically three 16-bit timers, and can be switched to different modes for timing or counting purposes.

## RTC/CMOS

The RTC interface provides a built-in clock to maintain the time of day and date, with the addition of 64 bytes of RAM to store data used for system configuration which can be accessed by the system BIOS. The configuration data can be modified using the 'set-up' facility provided during the boot process. Caution is strongly advised when accessing set-up. Incorrect configuration can prevent the system from booting up.

# Disk drives

*OPERATING PRINCIPLES*

From the earliest days of computer technology, mass storage media have been essential, e.g. paper tape, magnetic tape, magnetic disk and optical disk. The floppy disk, or diskette, was probably one of the most important developments, and for some of the first PCs it was the only storage medium available; it still is an efficient method of distributing data and software. Hard disk drives, sometimes called *fixed disk drives*, have now become an absolute necessity on the modern PC, mainly because of the increased size of modern software, and increased pressure to reduce the time taken to access data.

It is necessary to spend some time looking at the basic terminology and operating principles associated with disk technology, which are common to both floppy and hard disk drives. The technology is based on that used in audio cassette and video tape recording equipment. The disk is coated in a magnetic oxide substance, the particles of which can be magnetized and arranged to represent sound, images or computer data. The magnetically coated material is constructed as a circular disk with a central hole called the drive hub or spindle access hole; this enables the disk to be clamped into the drive and rotated at high speed. The disk is housed in a protective environment: the diskette in a plastic sleeve, the hard disk in a sealed case.

Simplified diagrams illustrated in Fig. 2.13 show (a) the main physical components of a hard disk drive, and (b) a functional block diagram including signal processing details.

The disk is spun by a small electric motor, the speed of which is controlled accurately by electronic feedback circuitry. A recording head, in close proximity to the disk surface, converts electrical signals into magnetic pulses that are recorded on to the disk's surface. The process of recording on to a disk is referred to as *writing*. Playback or *reading* the data is achieved as the disk passes the read/write head converting the magnetic pulses on the disk back into electrical signals. Most disk drives now use more than one read/write head in order to access both sides of the disk or to access more than one disk, as with most hard disk drives.

The heads, of which there are two or more, are mounted on to a movable bracket called the actuator, which positions the heads precisely over the disk under the direction of the disk controller. This controller is also used to control the flow of data between the disk drive and the computer bus system.

Inside the PC-clone an adaptor card plugging into an expansion slot provides a method of connecting the disk drive to the system board, and serves both floppy and hard disk drives. Adaptor cards are often multipurpose devices providing additional facilities such as input/output ports for printer, mouse, joystick and modem. The current trend is for manufacturers to mount the disk drive connectors directly on the system board, as many compatible manufacturers have done for some time.

(a)

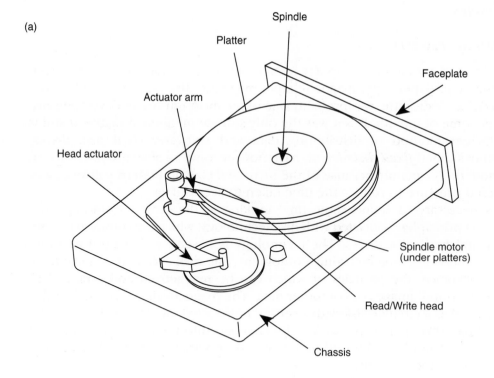

(b)

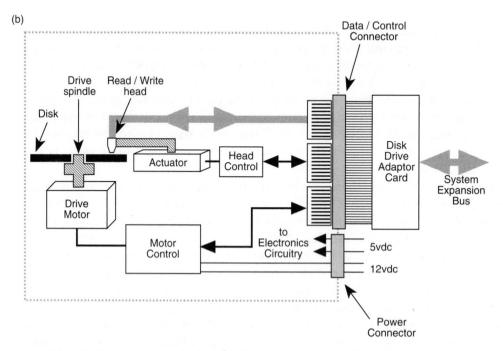

**Fig. 2.13** (a) Components of a disk drive; (b) disk drive block diagram

*STRUCTURE OF A DISK*

The structure used for storing data on a disk brings with it a range of technical terms that needs to be understood for later work in system configuration, particularly for hard disk drives.

The data written on to a disk are organized in a particular way. The surface of the disk is divided magnetically into a number of concentric rings called tracks, as shown in Fig. 2.14(a). The number of tracks on a diskette is typically 80, but for hard disks it can be over 1000.

Figure 2.14(b) shows how the surface is also divided radially into sectors, as in pieces of a pie. Diskettes typically divide each track into 9 or 18 sectors, and hard disks from 17 to over 100. Each individual sector of a track stores 512 bytes ($\frac{1}{2}$ Kb) of data, and its precise position is identified by the side of the disk, the track, and the sector, as shown in Fig. 2.14(c).

The total capacity of a disk can be calculated using the following equation:

(No. of sides, heads or surfaces) $\times$ (No. of tracks) $\times$ (No. of sectors) $\times$ $\frac{1}{2}$ Kb

For example: a $3\frac{1}{2}$ inch HD diskette has two heads, 80 tracks/side, and 18 sectors:

$$\text{Total capacity} = 2 \times 80 \times 18 \times \tfrac{1}{2}\,\text{Kb}$$
$$= \textbf{1.44 Mb}$$

*DISK DRIVE CONNECTORS*

In order to function, most disk drives need two supply voltages: 12 V for the motor, and 5 V for the electronic circuitry. The power supply leads shown earlier in the chapter (see Fig. 2.8), are pushed into connectors at the rear of the drive as illustrated in Fig. 2.15.

In addition to the power cable, another cable is needed to link the disk drive and system board adaptor card for data and control signals. The cable used is *ribbon cable*, and usually has three individual connectors, one for the adaptor card, and the others permitting the connection of two disk drives.

# Floppy disk drive

The twin-drive cable used for $3\frac{1}{2}$ inch floppy disk drives is illustrated in Fig. 2.16. If a single disk drive is to be used, then the end connector after the cable twist is connected to the drive which is identified as drive A:. When a second drive is added, there is a need to distinguish it from the first. This is achieved by connecting to the second connector which is used to identify this drive as B:. Some manufacturers use ribbon cable without a twist, in which case, drive A: identity is selected using the jumpers on each individual drive. With some older systems there are additional tasks to be performed when installing drives, which are discussed in more detail in Chapter 8 – Practical Exercises and Upgrading Guides.

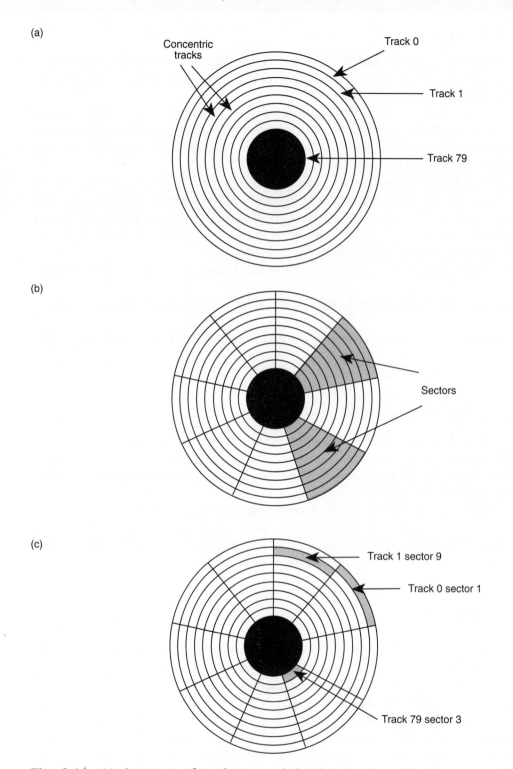

**Fig. 2.14** (a) Structure of tracks on a disk; (b) structure of sectors on a disk; (c) identification of sectors

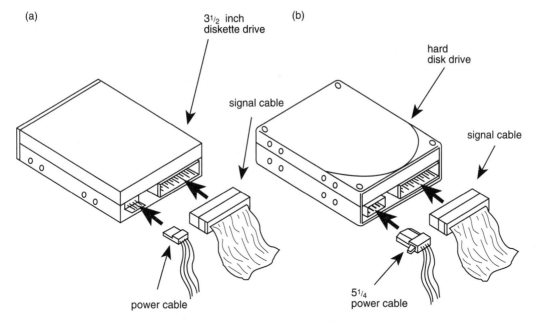

**Fig. 2.15**   Power connector for (a) floppy disk drive; (b) hard disk drive

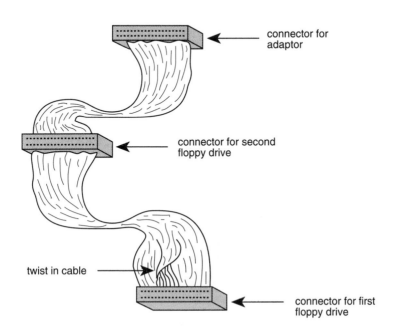

**Fig. 2.16**   Twin 3½ inch floppy disk drive cable

The diskette used in a floppy disk drive is removable, and there are two popular sizes: $3\frac{1}{2}$ inch and $5\frac{1}{4}$ inch. The sizes refer to the overall dimensions of the protective sleeve. The diagrams in Fig. 2.17 illustrate the overall construction.

Figure 2.17(b) shows the basic construction of a $5\frac{1}{4}$ inch diskette. The head aperture is an elongated hole in the protective sleeve allowing head access to

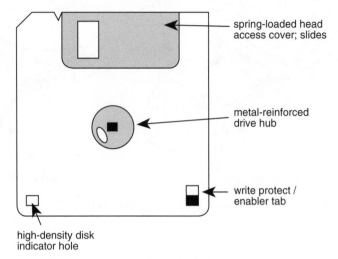

Fig. 2.17(a)   A $3\frac{1}{2}$ inch diskette

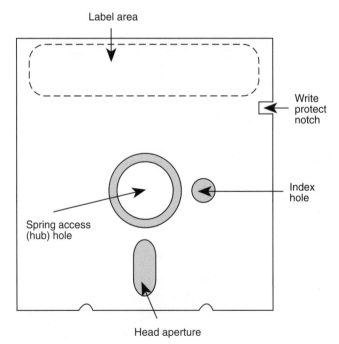

Fig. 2.17(b)   A $5\frac{1}{4}$ inch diskette

the disk. This is an area of the disk that is particularly vulnerable to damage when handled without care. The index hole was used on older systems to determine the precise position of the disk as it rotated; this is achieved on modern systems magnetically without using the index hole. The disk can be write-protected, preventing the user from writing to or *formatting* the disk, by covering the write-protect notch. When this notch is uncovered a switch or 'electronic eye' is activated in the drive, allowing full use.

Making your $3^1/_2$ inch diskette read-only is a little simpler. As shown in Fig. 2.17(a) a slider button replaces the notch. When the slider covers the hole, full access to the disk provides read and write facilities. When the hole is open, the disk is write-protected. This should not be mistaken for the hole in the adjacent corner of the diskette used to indicate a high-density disk (1.44 Mb). The access cover protects the disk surface and automatically slides to the side, enabling head access when the disk starts to spin.

Each of the diskettes is available in different formats, owing to continued developments in manufacturing technology. The most popular at present are the $3^1/_2$ inch 1.44 Mb, and the $5^1/_4$ inch 1.2 Mb, although the latest $3^1/_2$ inch 2.88 Mb is gaining some popularity. Table 2.1 details the differences between each of the standard formats.

**Table 2.1**  Diskette formats

| Format | Capacity | Heads(sides) | Tracks/side | Sectors/track | Bytes/sector |
|--------|----------|--------------|-------------|---------------|--------------|
| $3^1/_2$ inch | 720 Kb | 2 | 80 | 9 | $^1/_2$ Kb |
| $3^1/_2$ inch | 1.44 Mb | 2 | 80 | 18 | $^1/_2$ Kb |
| $3^1/_2$ inch | 2.88 Mb | 2 | 80 | 36 | $^1/_2$ Kb |
| $5^1/_4$ inch | 360 Kb | 2 | 40 | 9 | $^1/_2$ Kb |
| $5^1/_4$ inch | 1.2 Mb | 2 | 80 | 15 | $^1/_2$ Kb |

# Hard disk drive

The hard disk drive contains several disks. Each disk is called a platter, and is constructed from solid metal, rather than plastic. The platters are arranged on top of each other, with sufficient space between them for the heads to operate. Each platter is double sided and consequently has two dedicated heads. This arrangement is shown in a simplified form in Fig. 2.18.

Before continuing, a word of warning:

- **The casing of a hard disk drive must never be opened: there are no user-serviceable parts inside!**

Unlike the diskettes used with a floppy disk drive, the disks in a hard drive are fixed permanently to the mechanism through a common drive spindle. This ensures that all are fixed in relation to each other, and rotate at the same speed.

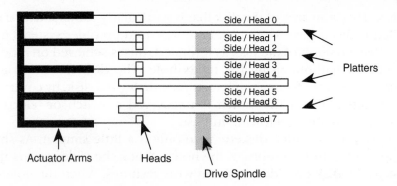

**Fig. 2.18**  Arrangement of platters in a hard disk drive

This arrangement provides an explanation of the alternative name used for a hard disk drive – fixed disk drive.

Disk heads are attached to the same actuator assembly, and cannot be positioned independently. The group of heads therefore accesses the same track number but on a different disk surface. The term used to describe a collection of tracks on all surfaces is a cylinder, i.e. the number of cylinders represents the number of tracks per surface.

This can be used in an example to determine the capacity of a hard disk that has 15 heads, 1632 cylinders, and 54 sectors/track, and stores $1/2$ Kb per sector:

(No. of sides, heads or surfaces) × (No. of tracks) × (No. of sectors) × $1/2$ Kb

Since the number of cylinders is in effect the number of tracks

$$capacity = 15 \times 1632 \times 54 \times 1/2 \text{ Kb}$$

$$= 676 \text{ Mb}$$

Although in principle all hard disk drives perform the same function in similar ways, there have been developments over the years resulting in different standards relating to the different controllers, encoding methods, and drive interfaces used.

*DISK DRIVE CONTROLLER*

The controller is an electronic circuit board that houses several chips and possibly a simple microprocessor with the role of go-between for the system board and drive.

The main functions of a controller are to convert data between different formats, to isolate the hardware from the software, and to match speed of operation between devices. Older hard disk drive controllers were based on adaptor cards used in the expansion slots, but as you will discover, modern drive controllers are mounted directly on to the drive itself.

**Table 2.2** Comparison of encoding methods

| To be encoded | FM | MFM | RLL |
|---|---|---|---|
| 0 0 | PN PN | PN PN | PN NN |
| 0 1 | PN PP | PN NP | NP NN |
| 1 0 0 | PP PN PN | NP NN PN | NN PN NN |

P describes a single pulse; N describes no pulse.

*ENCODING METHODS*

Encoding is a method of representing digital signals with a series of coded pulses. In its simplest format, '1' could be represented by a single pulse, and '0' by no pulse. This creates problems if there are long series of zeros since the drive can lose its way. An improved method might be to use two pulses to represent '1', and a pulse followed by no pulse to represent '0'. Examples include FM, MFM, and RLL. Confused? Don't worry, you only need to be aware that different methods of encoding exist.

Frequency modulation (FM) and modified frequency modulation (MFM) differ in the code that is used to represent '0' and '1'. MFM became standard for several years but was improved upon in the 1980s with a new method called run length limited (RLL). This introduced a more complex encoding method which effectively reduced the number of pulses needed and boosted the capacity of a disk drive by at least 50%. It may be interesting to note that the majority of floppy disk drives use MFM as an encoding method.

Table 2.2 provides a comparison of encoding methods used to represent '00', '01' and '100'. Do not feel intimidated by this, the manufacturer looks after all of the detail. The table is designed to show that the more complex methods actually use fewer pulses, which for technical reasons leads to increased efficiency. As can be seen, using RLL, only one pulse is needed to represent '100', compared to four pulses for the outdated FM method.

*DRIVE INTERFACES*

Encoding is sometimes confused with the functions performed by an interface. The definition of interface includes both hardware and software, and can be thought of as the 'language' that enables the drive and controller to communicate. Examples include ST506, ESDI, IDE, EIDE and SCSI.

The early ST506 (Shugart Technologies), and ESDI (enhanced small device interface) interfaces are not used in modern systems, and your only chance of seeing one is in an old system used for simple tasks. The popular standard used for many years was the ST506, which was only replaced by the ESDI to improve on inherent limitations. Both interface connections were easily identified by the two cables interconnecting the disk drive and controller card. These are shown in Fig. 2.19. A 20-wire ribbon cable was used for data transfer, and a 34-wire cable

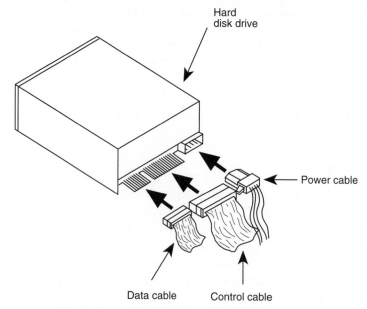

Hard
disk drive

Power cable

Data cable          Control cable

**Fig. 2.19**   ST506 drive cables for data and control

for control signals. Although similar cables were used for both the ST506 and the ESDI, the interfaces were neither electrically compatible nor interchange-able. Both interfaces could accommodate MFM and RLL encoding methods.

A wealth of information exists in a whole range of older PC books discussing these earlier interfaces, their applications, setting up and installation. The information available will include references to selection of drives, the addition of terminating resistors used to simulate a drive connection, and the labelling of drives C and D. Reference has been made here to some of the earlier devices to help existing users to differentiate between these and later devices. All modern domestic systems use the IDE interface, possibly SCSI, or something similar, so the present discussion of ST506 and ESDI ends here.

*ATA-IDE INTERFACE*

Limitations imposed by these early interfaces led to the development of the popular systems used in today's PCs. Recognizing that a significant limitation was the distance between drive and controller, an interface was developed by Compaq and Western Digital that involved mounting the controller directly on to the drive. Designed to interface easily with the ISA *expansion bus*, the integrated drive electronics (IDE) interface results in a single 40-way ribbon cable running from the IDE drive/controller to a simple adaptor card. This card is really nothing more than a connector providing easy access to the system bus. This single 40-wire ribbon cable helps to identify the IDE drive/controller.

The extension to the 16-bit ISA bus used with IDE drives is commonly referred to as an AT attachment (ATA), ATA interface, or ATA-IDE interface. It has proved to be very popular on modern domestic systems and has been adopted as an industry-wide standard.

In general, ATA-IDE drives are easier to install than their earlier counterparts. With the controller mounted on the drive, connection is relatively simple. There are six basic steps to the installation:

1. Install an adaptor card if not present or not available on the system board.
2. Fix the drive into the bay provided.
3. Connect the power lead to the drive.
4. Connect the 40-way interface ribbon cable between the drive and adaptor (or system board).
5. Use 'set-up' to inform the system of the drive's presence and type.
6. Prepare the drive for use, i.e. *partitioning* and *formatting*.

The IDE interface is limited to the installation of two hard disk drives, and the standard AT BIOS limited to 63 sectors/track and 1024 cylinders. This results in a maximum capacity per drive of 528 Mb. The standard IDE has been extended to increase this capacity, resulting in the enhanced IDE interface (EIDE).

EIDE allows for a different method to the traditional cylinder/sector address-ing technique by using logical block addressing (LBA). LBA is a scheme used to count individual blocks of data from the start of the drive. The only limit is on the number of block address locations that can be identified on the disk. At the time of writing, this can result in capacities in the region of 8.4 Gb. EIDE also allows the addition of a second IDE channel with specific support for CD-ROM drives, and up to four drives in total.

EIDE is now very popular on new PCs and can be distinguished from IDE by four main features:

- access to drive capacities greater than 528 Mb
- access to more than two drives
- connection of devices other than hard disk drives
- increase in the data *transfer rate*.

In order to use EIDE, the system needs to use a BIOS and OS that recognize the interface and drive requirements. If not, there are three methods of overcoming the difficulty: by either upgrading the BIOS to one that supports more than 528 Mb and incorporates LBA, using a host adaptor designed to support more than 528 Mb, or using the special software supplied by some manufacturers.

Installation of ATA drives is discussed further in Chapter 8 – Practical Exercises and Upgrading Guides.

*SCSI*

Pronounced 'scuzzy' the small computer systems interface (SCSI) essentially provides an expansion BUS on to which up to eight devices, including the host computer, can be connected. The controller is mounted on the drive, and internally uses a single ribbon cable to link with the adaptor card. As with EIDE, the SCSI can be used with devices other than hard disk drives, and used with very high capacities. One advantage in its use is the relatively simple method that can be used to add SCSI devices internally, or externally to the system base unit.

Installed in one of the expansion slots or part of the system board, the internal SCSI host connection uses a similar single connecting cable as the ATA-IDE interface. External peripherals can be added through a SCSI port made available on the rear of the base unit.

There are special requirements when installing SCSI drives, such as selecting each device's unique SCSI identification, but since the majority of domestic PCs currently use ATA-IDE or EIDE, the SCSI will not be discussed further.

## CD-ROM

*OPERATING PRINCIPLES*

CD-ROM is basically an adaptation of the compact disk technology used in domestic stereo systems. Contrary to the assumption you might make from the name, it is possible to write to a CD-ROM with the appropriate equipment. CD-ROM disks store data in the same way as the audio CD player, except that instead of up to 75 minutes of music, the disk provides storage for 680 Mb of data or software. The most popular application for CD-ROM currently is that of mixing sounds and images for multimedia applications.

The CD-ROM uses light instead of magnetism. The data are stored as a pattern of black and white spots that are read using a photodetector and reflected laser light. The principle is similar to that of the barcode reader at your local supermarket checkout.

Instead of concentric tracks as used with magnetic disks, the CD has one very long continuous spiral, much like the pattern of the groove on a record. This spiral starts at the outer edge and extends almost to the centre. As it is scanned from the centre outwards, the speed of the CD is varied depending on position, i.e. the CD spins faster towards the centre so that the same length of track moves under the read/write head every second.

This continuous spiral is divided into sectors called large frame units, which are the basis for addressing. The standard used for CD-ROM uses a large frame unit with 2352 bytes, which are divided into data storage, addressing, synchronization and auxiliary purposes. A typical example would use 2048 bytes for the data field, 4 bytes for the addressing field, 12 bytes for the synchronization field, and 288 bytes for the auxiliary field. This arrangement is referred to as data mode one, and is one of several modes used for different arrangements of fields.

Large frame units are grouped into sections or tracks spaced by gaps in a similar pattern to that of individual sound tracks on a record. The CD is organized with up to 99 tracks, each of which consists of at least 300 large frame units, and each of which must be used solely for data, audio or video.

**Table 2.3** Comparison of floppy, hard and CD-ROM disk drives

|  | Floppy disk drive | Hard disk drive | CD-ROM drive |
|---|---|---|---|
| Storage medium | Magnetic | Magnetic | Optical/light |
| Format | Concentric tracks divided into sectors | | Single spiral track divided into sectors |
| Capacity | Up to 2.88 Mb | Over 16 Gb | 680 Mb |
| Speed | Constant 300–600 rpm | Constant 3600 rpm | Variable depending on position |
| *Access time* |  | 9–30 ms | 100–200 ms on modern designs |
| *Transfer rate* | 50 Kb/s | 500–5000 Kb/s | Single speed:    150 Kb/s<br>Double speed:    300 Kb/s<br>Quad. speed:    600 Kb/s<br>×8 speed    1.2 Mb/s |

Physically, CD-ROM drives are fairly standard, typically using the same space as a 5$\frac{1}{4}$ inch floppy disk drive, and using the same types of connectors as a hard disk drive. The significant difference for the user is the method by which the CD is inserted into the drive. Some drives have an opening drawer into which the CD is placed, while others use a caddy, which is a protective plastic carrier. When inserted into the drive, a shutter in the caddy opens automatically to provide access for the read/write head. This system has the advantage of giving additional protection to your CDs during handling, but the disadvantage of additional cost. Protection of your CDs when handled is important; contrary to popular belief they can be scratched and made unusable. CD-ROMs are now used extensively for transferring large amounts of data and large programs between systems.

Table 2.3 provides a comparison of the floppy disk, hard disk and CD-ROM drives in terms of main characteristics.

*MULTIMEDIA*

'Multi' means 'more than one', but the word 'medium' (the singular of media) is not to be found in the thesaurus on your PC. Look it up! When you look up the word 'media' in your good old-fashioned dictionary it will provide an explanation similar to 'newspapers and broadcasting as conveying information to the public'. The word 'medium' will result in 'surroundings in which a thing exists or is produced'. In connection with PCs, the term 'media' describes the different ways in which information, whether it be audio, video or digital, can be stored and used. The modern PC has the power to handle not only traditional computer data, but also audio and video. To most people an upgrade to multimedia means the addition of a CD-ROM drive to handle the large amounts of data, and a *sound card* to cope with audio that goes far beyond the traditional beeps and whistles of older systems.

Most PCs being purchased for either home or industrial use are now multimedia PCs (MPCs). The term multimedia in this context means the mixing together of sound, video, graphics and other digital information, and making it available on your PC.

The potential for the multimedia PC is tremendous. Although games form a major part of many commercial retailing activities, the use of the MPC for training, teaching and education, with links to virtual reality, has generated high expectations for the coming years.

The current multimedia standard relies on the following recommended system requirements:

- microprocessor 80386DX or better
- at least 8 Mb of RAM
- $3^{1}/_{2}$ inch floppy disk drive
- hard disk drive at least 200 Mb
- quad-speed CD-ROM drive
- SVGA video display
- sound card
- game port
- MIDI port
- system software Microsoft Windows 3.1 or later with appropriate multimedia extensions.

## Summary

This chapter has covered many of the components that make up the system base unit in a modern PC. You should now feel a little more familiar with the power supply, the system board, the microprocessor, memory, disk drives, and CD-ROMs. Although the jargon used is essential, you may also feel a little confused by some of the terminology used. At this stage this is to be expected, but with some further reading and a little practical work, things will soon become clearer. Use the self-assessment questions in the final section of this chapter to refresh your memory and to help to develop your understanding.

## Self-assessment questions

1. Explain the following terms:
   (a) integrated circuit
   (b) voltage
   (c) RAM
   (d) bus
   (e) tower system
   (f) sector
   (g) large frame unit
   (h) platter
   (i) FRU
   (j) system clock

2. Describe the main purpose of each of the following:
   (a) microprocessor
   (b) system BIOS
   (c) expansion slot
   (d) keyboard controller
   (e) integrated support chip
   (f) disk drive controller
   (g) CMOS RAM
   (h) read/write head
   (i) stand-off
   (j) IDE interface

3. List the precautions necessary when working on a PC with the cover removed.

4. Sketch the layout of 'tracks' and 'sectors' on (a) a typical floppy disk; (b) a CD-ROM.

5. Sketch a typical system board (motherboard) showing all of the main components.

## Answers

Relevant reading material is indicated below by the page number corresponding to the question.

1. (a) page 15
   (b) page 10
   (c) page 18
   (d) page 15
   (e) page 7
   (f) page 25
   (g) page 34
   (h) pages 24, 29
   (i) page 7
   (j) page 20

2. (a) page 15
   (b) page 19
   (c) page 19
   (d) page 20
   (e) page 21
   (f) page 30
   (g) page 18
   (h) page 23
   (i) page 15
   (j) pages 31, 32

3. page 7

4. (a) page 26
   (b) page 34

5. page 16

## Basic jargon

*a.c.* Alternating current refers to a current that periodically reverses direction several times per second. The domestic mains supply is alternating current and varies 50 times per second (50 Hz).

*Access time.* The time taken to write or read data from a storage device. Measured in fractions of a second: ms, millisecond (thousandth of a second); μs, microsecond (millionth of a second); and ns, nanosecond (thousandth of a microsecond).

*Adaptor.* An electronic circuit board used to extend the system capabilities. Usually the card plugs into an expansion slot on the system board.

*Adaptor card.* See *Adaptor*.

*Address bus.* Bus used specifically for transferring address information.

*Block diagram.* A diagram that is used to give an outline of how a system works, using boxes to represent processes within the system.

*Bus.* A collection of electrical connections or pathways, along which electrical signals move.

*Bus mastering.* A device that can take over the system bus from the micro-processor to control the flow of data.

*Cache.* A special type of very high speed RAM used to store data and instructions used regularly by the microprocessor.

*Chip.* Another term for *Integrated circuit*.

*Chipset.* A collection of chips designed to work together in a PC with a particular microprocessor.

*CMOS set-up.* See *Set-up*.

*Compatible PC.* A system that is software compatible, but is significantly different in its hardware to the extent of not being able to use standard components freely.

*Control bus.* Bus used specifically for transferring control signals.

*CPU.* The central processing unit is also referred to as the processor or microprocessor and can be thought of as the 'brains' of the computer. It is discussed in more detail in Chapter 3.

*Crystal oscillator.* An electronic circuit producing a constant alternating signal. The 'crystal' is a small piece of quartz crystal housed in a metal can that is used to regulate the frequency of the oscillator.

*Current.* An electrical term used to describe the flow of electricity. Can be thought of as tiny particles flowing through a wire or circuit.

*d.c.* Direct current refers to current that, although it may vary, flows in one direction only. Batteries supply, and electronic circuits use direct current.

*Data bus.* Bus used specifically for transferring data.

*Drive bay.* The slot where disk and CD-ROM drives are mounted.

*Expansion bus.* An extension to the system bus that enables the expansion of the system using expansion or adaptor cards.

*Expansion card.* See *Adaptor card.*

*Expansion slot.* The system board socket that allows access to the expansion bus.

*Fixed-disk drive.* Another term for a hard disk drive.

*Formatting.* A process of introducing magnetic tracks on to a floppy or hard disk.

*FRU.* A field replaceable unit is a module or component of the system that can be replaced relatively easily, and for economic reasons is normally not worth repairing as a unit, e.g. floppy disk drive.

*Integrated circuit.* An electronic circuit built on to a tiny, single piece of silicon material, encased in resin. The circuit can contain from a few components to several million, depending on the scale of integration.

*Microprocessor.* In modern microcomputer systems using highly integrated components the CPU is referred to as the microprocessor.

*Modem.* A peripheral device commonly used for connection to the telephone or similar network.

*Motherboard.* Another term used to describe the system board.

*Partitioning.* A process of dividing the physical structure of a hard disk drive into one or more logical drives.

*PC-clone.* A system that is both hardware and software compatible with the IBM AT standard. This means that a clone will operate software in the same way, and that hardware components are usually interchangeable. Care must be taken because although some components appear to be suitable, sometimes they are electrically incompatible and will not operate correctly.

*Port.* An inlet/outlet from the system used to connect peripheral devices, often via connectors on the rear panel. A parallel port transfers data several bits at once, whereas a serial port transfers one bit after another. Serial ports are therefore slower in operation. The parallel port is usually used for connection to a printer, and the serial port for a mouse or modem.

*Reading.* The recovery of information from a storage device.

*'Ready' signal.* A signal used by a chip to indicate its readiness to transmit or receive data or instructions.

*Rectifier.* An electronic device that allows electric current to flow in one direction only. Used to convert a.c. into d.c.

*Register.* An area within the microprocessor for temporary storage of data, address codes or operating instructions.

*Regulator.* An electronic device used to prevent unwanted variations in output voltage.

*'Reset' signal.* A signal used to 'restart' processes within a chip. An example includes the reset button on your PC which performs a soft-boot of the system.

*Ribbon cable.* An electrical cable formed by combining several individual wires side-by-side to form the appearance of a ribbon.

*Set-up.* The term set-up is made with reference to the CMOS set-up program which can be accessed during the boot process. It enables modification of the CMOS settings for configuration information.

*Sound card.* An adaptor card used in multimedia systems to enhance the sound produced.

*Switch mode power supply.* A special type of power supply used in modern domestic equipment that effectively operates by switching on and off several thousand times per second. The d.c. output voltage is controlled by the rate at which the supply switches.

*System board.* An electronic circuit board that forms the base for the main components of the system. Components are mounted either directly on to the board, or through the addition of plug-in expansion cards.

*System bus.* A term used to describe the data, address and control buses collectively.

*Tape streamer.* Typically a high-quality, high-capacity tape recorder used to back-up the programs and files from a hard disk drive or other large storage device.

*Transfer rate.* The rate at which data can be transferred. Measured in Kb/s, or Mb/s depending on the type of device.

*Transformer.* A device made from multiple windings of wire on a metal core, and used to convert an alternating voltage into an alternating voltage of different value.

*VLSI.* Very large scale integration is used to describe the level of integration of individual components, such as transistors, on to a single chip. VLSI refers to a technology that puts over 10 000 circuit components on to a single chip.

*Voltage.* An electrical term used to describe the driving force in an electrical circuit. Measured in volts, most people should be aware of the significant difference between the driving forces of the 240 V mains supply and a 6 V battery.

*Writing.* The saving of information to a storage device.

# 3
# The microprocessor

## Inside the chip

The microprocessor performs most of the system's calculating and processing functions. The diagram in Fig. 3.1, and following explanations, will give you a basic understanding of the operation of the microprocessor. Much of the complexity of the circuitry has been omitted to keep the explanations simple, but it must be remembered that these devices are very sophisticated and their operation should not be treated lightly.

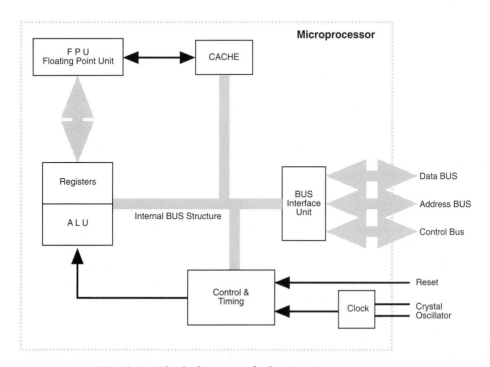

**Fig. 3.1** Block diagram of a basic microprocessor

Operations involved in the microprocessor can be represented in seven basic functions:

- *arithmetic and logic unit (ALU)*
- registers
- control and timing
- clock
- bus interface unit
- floating point unit
- internal cache.

### ARITHMETIC AND LOGIC UNIT

The ALU effectively handles the decision-making processes. As the name implies these involve arithmetic functions such as addition and subtraction, and logic functions such as bit comparison and logical-AND. Instructions are decoded from the control unit, and either carried out directly or used to execute codes to modify data in registers.

### REGISTERS

Registers within the microprocessor can be thought of as a number of areas for the temporary storage of data, address codes, and operating instructions. When current data are kept in a register that operates much more quickly than main memory, the microprocessor is not slowed down during accessing. The register width also plays a significant part in increasing the performance of a modern PC. The greater the number of bits stored in a register, the more information can be processed in every microprocessor *clock cycle*. Modern 64-bit registers have the potential to improve the microprocessor's performance eight-fold compared to processors using 8-bit registers.

Some registers are used for general-purpose operations, but others may be dedicated to particular functions, e.g. specifically for data storage, or for remembering the current step in an instruction.

### CONTROL AND TIMING

Some type of control unit must be provided for the control and timing of operations within the entire microprocessor chip. Depending on the type of processor, this unit may have variations in function and the terminology used, but is always responsible for synchronizing the movement of data within the microprocessor, and management of both external and internal control signals. Stepping through the instructions within a program produces a control need for timing pulses usually generated by a dedicated clock source or the system clock. Using clock pulses in this way leads to the circuitry being referred to as *clocked logic*.

## CLOCK

The clock circuitry provides the synchronization pulses used to ensure that the individual parts of the processor operate together. The clock driver derives the pulses from the main system clock and may vary in frequency depending on the type of processor.

The term clock cycle is used to refer to the duration in which the clock pulse goes through a complete cycle of 'ON' and 'OFF'. This is an important concept since many of the improvements in microprocessor architecture have been aimed at increasing the number of instructions that can be carried out during one clock cycle.

## BUS INTERFACE UNIT

The bus interface unit, or bus controller, connects and controls the data, address and control lines between the system bus and the processor. Outputs from the processor are decoded to generate bus and control signals which ensure the correct flow of data and address information across the system bus.

## FLOATING POINT UNIT

The floating point unit (FPU) is a coprocessor that can be thought of as an assistant processor. It is only active when instructions related to complex mathematics are processed, and traditionally is referred to as the maths coprocessor. The FPU is likely to benefit a system using maths-intensive software such as CAD and spreadsheet packages. The unit is effectively wired in parallel with the microprocessor adding several specialist registers to its capacity. On early system boards (prior to 486SX) a coprocessor was based external to the microprocessor in a separate chip. In 486DX-based and later systems, these facilities are incorporated within the microprocessor chip itself. The FPU is not the only type of coprocessor to be found. A whole range of specialist coprocessors is available to assist with tasks such as handling video images using specialized compression techniques, and tasks associated with communications and error checking.

## INTERNAL CACHE

Internal cache is essential to efficient operation of the modern microprocessor. Very high speed SRAM, internal to the processor chip, allows frequently used data and instructions to be stored on-chip, thus reducing access to the external bus. In earlier processors the internal cache was used for a range of different functions, but in modern chips, separate dedicated cache is used for data and for instructions. This dedicated cache is referred to as *primary* or *first-level (L1) cache* to distinguish it from general-purpose system board cache which is called *secondary* or *second-level (L2) cache*. It should not be assumed that L2 or secondary cache is always external to the processor: in the most recent microprocessors L2 cache is internal to the processor chip. This memory hierarchy of different levels is discussed further in Chapter 5 – Memory.

*PACKAGING*

Modern microprocessor packages are compact and usually square. Contacts are placed around the four sides, either along the edge, or underneath. Several styles of packaging can be produced with different connecting arrangements depending on whether the chip is mounted in a socket or soldered directly on to the surface of the system board (*surface mount technology*).

A popular package is the pin grid array (PGA), shown in Fig. 3.2. It has an inner and outer square of solid pins on its underside, and is designed to insert into specially produced sockets. Size varies depending on the number of pins to be accommodated. The latest design of PGA is the staggered pin grid array (SPGA), in which some of the pins are offset, and their alignment is staggered to increase the density.

If not handled carefully pins can be damaged, so some chip manufacturers have developed pinless packages such as the leadless chip carrier and plastic quad flatpack.

The leadless chip carrier (LCC) resembles a small ceramic tile with the bottom edge striped with gold-plated contact pads, illustrated in Fig. 3.3. The LCC is designed to be used in sockets, whereas a similar design, the plastic leadless chip carrier (PLCC), can also be mounted directly on to the circuit board using surface-mount techniques.

The quad flat package (QFP), or plastic quad flat package (PQFP) is sometimes called simply the 'quad flat pack' and is shown in Fig. 3.4. The chips are compact, low cost, and designed to be soldered flat against the surface of the circuit board. The soldering involved limits use of the package to low-power devices.

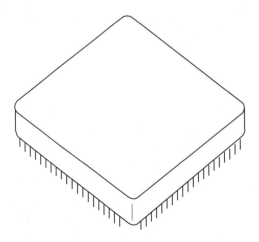

**Fig. 3.2**   Pin grid array (PGA) package

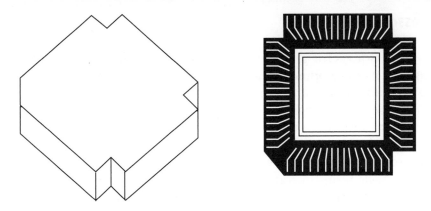

**Fig. 3.3** Leadless chip carrier (LCC) package

As microprocessors continue to become more complex, and packaging requirements change, manufacturers continue to improve on design. In addition to the more standard packaging, the latest Intel Pentium microprocessor is available to computer manufacturers in a package referred to as a tape carrier package (TCP). This design offers large pin capacity and small size, yet maintains electrical and thermal performance. The package has very small leads arranged around the edge in a similar way to the PQFP and is surface mounted on to the circuit board. Definitely not one for replacement by the user armed with a medium-sized screwdriver and big hammer!

**Fig. 3.4** Quad flat package (QFP)

# Microprocessor developments

The microprocessor is crucial in determining the performance of a modern PC, and throughout its development manufacturers have worked towards improvements in speed and addressing capabilities. The steps taken in microprocessor design during the past 10 years are better described as leaps in technology. The unfortunate amateur or even the experienced professional can have difficulty in keeping up with the developments and technical terms introduced to describe these new circuits and functions within a microprocessor chip.

Some of the basic terms introduced as chips have developed from the 80286 into the Pentium Pro are discussed in the following pages.

*OPERATING MODES*

The *operating modes* associated with the development of microprocessors include three true operating modes and one quasi-operating mode:

- real-address mode
- protected mode
- virtual-8086 mode
- system management mode (SMM).

These reflect the developments achieved over the last decade. Real-address mode is very much a part of the 8086 processor, and protected mode was introduced with the 80286. Both virtual-8086 and SMM relate primarily to the modern processors of today. In order to maintain backward compatibility most modern microprocessors offer all of the first three modes, with SMM provided as a standard feature on systems that are designed for reduced power consumption.

Real-address mode provides an operating environment similar to that of the original 8086 microprocessor with all of the original limitations. Operation of the processor is limited to 20 address lines allowing access to only 1 Mb of physical memory, in 64 Kb segments. The processor is placed in this mode following power-up or a reset.

Protected mode was originally introduced with the 80286 and was designed to overcome some of the 8086 limitations. Using 24 address lines, up to 16 Mb of physical memory can be accessed in which segments can be protected from each other, thus enabling multiple tasks to run simultaneously. In this mode all instructions are available, so that the highest performance is provided.

Virtual-8086 mode is really a mode within protected mode and allows the processor to run 8086 software in a protected environment with multitasking capabilities. Memory can be partitioned into sections, in which different operating systems and applications can run without interference.

SMM is not truly an operating mode, but a method for implementing power management in which unused parts of the processor or computer can be shut down, hence conserving power. Although becoming popular in desktop systems, SMM was originally produced for use with battery-operated systems such as notebooks and laptops.

*PIPELINES*

Areas of a chip designed to process data and instructions (the ALU is an example) are increasingly being referred to as *execution units*. An execution unit with the ability to process more than one instruction per clock cycle is called a *pipeline*. Pipelines execute integer instructions in several stages. Typical stages in a modern processor will include prefetch, decode, execute and write-back.

'Prefetch' describes the action of fetching an instruction from memory, and 'decode' is the stage of converting the code into a sequence of operations ready for execution. 'Execute' is the stage in which the necessary actions are carried out, and the 'write-back' stage is when results are stored back in memory. Several instructions can be processed at the same time but at different stages, and passed along the pipeline through the chip. Currently the processing of two integer instructions per pipeline clock cycle is common in processors such as the 80486 and Pentium.

As a result of decision-making processes in the software program, problems can arise with pipelines due to branching. A pipeline can be loaded with instructions assuming a particular direction for the program to follow. If events redirect the program along a different branch, the contents of the pipeline must be discarded, resulting in wasted time. The larger the pipeline, the more time might be wasted through branching within the program.

*BRANCH PREDICTION LOGIC*

Branch prediction logic is a technology adopted in modern microprocessors in which the processor predicts the most likely branch to be taken in a program as it is filling the pipeline. The purpose of branch prediction logic is to keep pipelines full for as much of the time as possible. Currently, these processor branch guesses are sufficiently correct to benefit overall performance.

*SUPERSCALAR ARCHITECTURE*

Superscalar architecture is used with reference to modern chip design. It is used basically to describe a microprocessor that contains more than one execution unit. A typical example to be discussed later in the chapter is that of the Pentium using two execution units (ALUs) in one chip. The principal of superscalar technology is not new; it has been in use from as early as 1964 in mainframe computers.

*BURST MODE*

In simple terms, blocks of data to be transferred are sent in one burst with the minimum of control signals. The destination of the first byte of data is specified, then the block of data is moved one byte after another, without intervention from the microprocessor. This means that the microprocessor can be engaged in other activities while transfers take place. Burst techniques have contributed significantly to the improved performance of modern system devices.

*PIPELINED BURST MODE*

Pipelined burst mode is used to describe a device such as cache that uses pipeline technology with burst-mode operation to transfer data.

*80286 MICROPROCESSOR*

The 80286 was a major step in processor design. The many improvements that made it superior to earlier processors included a 16-bit data bus, with 16-bit internal registers, 24 address lines, and internal circuitry that enabled faster operating speeds.

Design restrictions imposed on the 80286 had to make use of software available for earlier XT systems which involved the use of an 8-bit data bus capacity and 20 address lines. The new 80286 not only needed to be 'backward compatible', i.e. to be compatible with these earlier 8-bit systems with only 20 address lines, but also had to be able to access the greater memory capacity provided through the additional four address lines. Intel's answer to the problem was to provide the 80286 with two different operating modes: real and protected. Remember that real mode simulated the operation of earlier microprocessors with the same limitations, and protected mode allowed the processor to access all 24 address lines and make full use of the 16 Mb memory capacity, with its multitasking capabilities.

The new protected mode of operation was slow to gain support from software producers for two basic reasons:

❏ Once switched to protected mode, the only way to return to real mode was to reset the processor with the resultant loss of data.
❏ The additional memory accessed in protected mode still operated in 64 Kb segments.

These limitations of an otherwise very successful microprocessor were not fully realized until the introduction of the 80386.

*80386 MICROPROCESSOR FAMILY*

Designed with full consideration for the growing PC market, the 80386 microprocessor was a true 32-bit device processing data 32 bits at a time, and accessing a full 32 address lines. The 32 address lines increased the possible capacity to a staggering 4 Gb of physical memory. More speed, greater capacity, and improved versatility were the key to building on the success of the '286.

The final limitation originally imposed by the 80286 was in the way in which memory was organized. With the '386, segments were no longer restricted to 64 Mb, but could be virtually any size, resulting in a new mode of operation. Virtual-8086 mode allows memory to be partitioned into sections, and the microprocessor to simulate several 8086 processors at the same time. The advantage of this is that entirely different programs can run simultaneously in each section of memory, providing real multitasking capabilities.

To maintain compatibility the 80386 is provided with all three modes of operation: real, protected and virtual-8086. The chip still boots up in real mode, but can be easily switched using software commands without resetting.

It should be noted that the new design of the 80386 meant that some software developed for the 80386 would not operate on a system using the 80286. Early users of these '286 systems soon became familiar with the on-screen message "needs 386 or later".

*'386DX.* The '386DX was effectively the first version in the 80386 family. The 80386DX was originally labelled simply the 80386. It was not until after the introduction of a cut-down version, the '386SX, that the name of the original design was changed to 80386DX.

*'386SX.* A cost-effective compromise, the '386SX has the same modes, and is internally very nearly identical to the '386DX, but is connected externally with only 16 data lines. This limitation produces a 'bottleneck' in the flow of data, and is responsible for a reduction in the overall speed of the system.

Figure 3.5 illustrates the main difference between the SX and DX versions. Both have 32 address lines, but the SX is limited to 16 data lines.

*'386SL.* The '386SL was operationally a full 32-bit '386DX device designed specifically to meet the needs of notebook computers. These basic needs are reduced power consumption and higher levels of integration to reduce size. This makes the SL chip different in several ways.

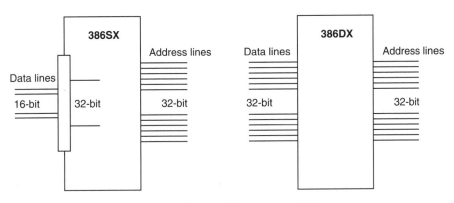

**Fig. 3.5** 386SX and DX external lines

The '386SL:

❏ uses SMM to conserve power
❏ is designed to work with a specific, dedicated input/output chip
❏ can operate at lower speeds, which also helps to reduce power.

*80486 MICROPROCESSOR FAMILY*

The '486 has total software compatibility with the '386, the same three operating modes, and the same 32-bit data and address buses. So what is the difference?

Improvements in the 80486 are derived from a complete redesign of the internal structure of the chip, allowing faster internal computing speeds when running at the same clock speed as earlier processors. The redesign included the following changes.

❏ Pipelining technology for the ALU.
❏ Reduced size of internal circuits resulting in shorter distances between internal components, and faster operation.
❏ Cache memory and controller. This provides fast, temporary storage which is responsible for a significant increase in processor speed. All '486 processors have 8 Kb of cache, apart from the DX4 which was upgraded to 16 Kb.
❏ FPU/maths coprocessor (DX versions), improving the speed for graphics and statistical packages.

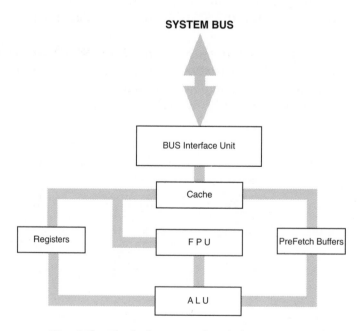

**Fig. 3.6**   Block diagram of 80486 microprocessor

The simplified block diagram in Fig. 3.6 illustrates the main functional blocks of the 80486 microprocessor, which include the ALU, FPU, registers, cache and bus interface unit. The operation of each block has been discussed earlier in the chapter and does not differ significantly from what has already been said. It should be remembered that the significant improvements in performance stem from the combination of units within one chip. A phrase comes to mind: "the sum of the whole is greater then the sum of the individuals".

The 80486 is available in SX and DX versions with the option of *clock multiplying*. The '486DX is basically that shown in the block diagram, and the SX version the same but stripped of the FPU. The clock-multiplying option comes in clock-doubling (DX2), and clock-tripling (DX4) versions.

*'486DX2.* The '486DX2 is effectively identical to the standard DX but with clock doubling, which means that internally the processor runs at twice the speed of the system board. Designed for high-speed internal operation, this does not affect the operation of external components. The '486DX2-66 provides a good example. The processor runs internally at 66 MHz, but is designed to run on a 33 MHz system board.

*'486DX4.* Not quite as the name might imply, the DX4 uses an internal clock tripler. Internally, the processor runs at three times the speed of the system board. At the time of development the opportunity was also taken to increase the size of the internal cache from the standard 8 Kb to 16 Kb. The '486DX4-75 is a 75 MHz processor designed to run on a 25 MHz system board.

*'486SL.* Deceptively, the '486SL microprocessor is a version of the '486DX adapted specifically for use in the notebook market. The '486SL is a highly integrated chip including memory controller and bus interface. With the addition of an external 82360SL input/output chip, virtually all of the requirements of a notebook PC are housed in two chips.

*'486 overdrive.* The '486 overdrive is basically a '486DX chip with internal clock-multiplying facilities, but designed specifically for upgrading systems originally produced for standard SX or DX versions. The main differences are in the packaging and pin-out design.

*THE PENTIUM*

Although the '80586' was anticipated for some time, it is generally accepted that because of copyright problems in the generic method of identifying microprocessors, i.e. '386, '486, this new product was labelled the Pentium. This provided some safeguards against wholesale copying by manufacturers other than Intel, but did not prevent manufacturers from producing versions of their own.

The Pentium processor architecture comprises all of the features of the Intel486 family with significant additions contributing to the processor's high performance. Those additional features include:

- superscalar architecture
- 64-bit data bus
- separate 8 Kb data and instruction caches
- branch prediction
- pipelined FPU
- voltage reduction technology (see *3.3 V processor*).

Figure 3.7 illustrates some of these new features in a simplified block diagram.

The superscalar architecture of the Intel Pentium processor includes two five-stage pipelines, each of which is effectively an execution unit (ALU). These are labelled the U and V pipelines, respectively, and each is capable of executing two instructions in parallel in a single clock cycle. This means that inside the processor chip four different instructions can be at different stages of execution, all at the same time. The five execution stages involved in each pipeline are prefetch, decode 1, decode 2, execute and write-back.

Connection to a 64-bit external data bus means that the Pentium processor can transfer data to and from memory at rates of up to 528 Mb/s. The addition

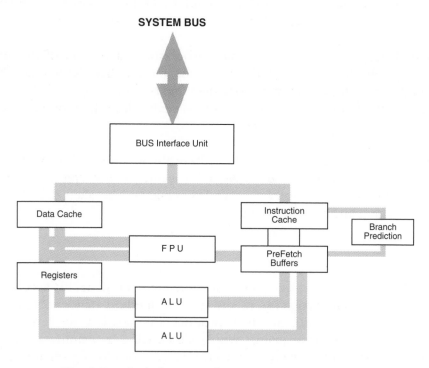

**Fig. 3.7**   Block diagram of Pentium microprocessor

of other features such as *bus cycle pipelining* which allows a second cycle to start before the first has finished, and burst mode operation improves performance still further.

The 16 Kb of cache used in the Pentium also provides significant improvements in several different ways.

❏ The 16 Kb cache is divided into two dedicated blocks, one for data and the other for program code.
❏ The method of organizing data in the cache is more efficient, the cache is divided into smaller 32-byte units, each of which can be searched relatively quickly.
❏ The cache controller has branch prediction capabilities.
❏ The data cache uses *write-back caching* techniques.

The separate caches allow simultaneous access, reducing conflict between data and instructions using cache. Write-back caching methods transfer data into cache without accessing main memory, and data are only written to memory when removed from cache. The alternative *write-through cache* transfers data to memory each time the processor writes to cache. Write-back caching techniques add to improved performance by reducing bus usage and preventing bottlenecks. Branch prediction boosts performance by predetermining the most likely instructions to be executed.

Finally, a three-stage pipelined FPU adds to the system performance with common instructions hard-wired on to the unit, i.e. addition, multiplication and division.

Pentium processors are available in a range of frequencies from 60 MHz to 166 MHz. The frequency usually quoted is the *core frequency* or internal chip frequency. Table 3.1 lists the range of Pentiums, their core frequencies, corresponding bus frequency, and operating voltages.

**Table 3.1**  Pentium frequencies and operating voltages

| Pentium | Core frequency (MHz) | Bus frequency (MHz) | Voltage (V) |
|---|---|---|---|
| P60 | 60 | 60 | 5 |
| P66 | 66 | 66 | 5 |
| P75 | 75 | 50 | 3.3 |
| P90 | 90 | 60 | 3.3 |
| P100 | 100 | 66 | 3.3 |
| P120 | 120 | 60 | 3.3 |
| P133 | 133 | 66 | 3.3 |
| P150 | 150 | 60 | 3.3 |
| P166 | 166 | 66 | 3.3 |

Chips produced from March 1993 were available in two speeds, 60 MHz and 66 MHz. The design difference was not intentional, but due to difficulties associated with manufacturing identical chips to such a high standard. Originally, the 60 MHz versions were those that when tested could not quite make the grade, but would happily operate at the lower frequency.

The high frequencies at which modern microprocessors operate bring with them additional problems. Compare a processor speed of 90 or 100 MHz with the frequency of radio stations found on the FM radio dial. Many local commercial stations transmit on frequencies in the range 90 to 100 MHz. The Pentium is a mini-transmitter, and as a result manufacturers must provide systems with appropriate screening, i.e. the metal case.

Factors like these are even more significant when you remind yourself of the relationship between size, heat and speed. The large, highly integrated chips of today produce great amounts of heat. Large numbers of transistors on a chip and high core frequencies result in high temperatures. Unfortunately, high temperatures have the affect of cutting speed, and this has led to an increase in the use of mini-fans for cooling. These not only reduce the risk of heat damage, but also help to maintain the performance of the processor.

"The Pentium is at least twice as fast as a 486DX2-66" or so we are led to believe from early advertising literature. In my experience, a more realistic figure might be 30% faster. Why the difference in opinion? For the Pentium to be more than twice as fast, the software program must make full use of the 16 Kb cache available, and must be easily separated to make full use of the two execution pipelines. The majority of software available at the moment cannot fully utilize either one, or both of these facilities, so in practice the Pentium's performance is lower than might be expected. At the time of publication, producers of software will be making much better use of the Pentium's powerful resources, resulting in much faster processing times.

Software is becoming increasingly available that has been designed specifically for the Pentium. Yes, it will run on a 486, and possibly a 386, but when running with a Pentium the software program instructions have been arranged to keep both the U and V pipelines busy at all times. In a Pentium this results in much faster execution.

As a summary to the inevitable comparison of 486-based and Pentium-based systems, Table 3.2 illustrates the main distinguishing features of a 486DX2-66 and a Pentium-66. The decision on what to buy? It depends on what you want!

*P24T*

The 486-based computers, advertised as "Pentium ready", are designed to use the P24T microprocessor as a direct replacement for the on-board 486 chip.

Will using the P24T to replace a '486 be faster? A little!

The P24T could be referred to as the Pentium-SX. Internally, the chip still has two processors and two pipelines and hence handles 64 bits, but externally it

**Table 3.2**  486DX2-66 vs Pentium-66

|  | 486DX2-66 | Pentium-66 |
|---|---|---|
| System frequency (MHz) | 33 | 66 |
| Core frequency (MHz) | 66 | 66 |
| Pipelines | 1 | 2 |
| Integral FPU | Yes | Yes |
| Internal cache | 8 Kb | 16 Kb |

connects only to a 32-bit bus (reminiscent of the 386SX and DX). This bottleneck prevents effective operation of the pipelining facilities, with the consequent reduction in speed of operation.

Figure 3.8 shows a simple comparison of the data connections used by (a) the '486, (b) the Pentium and (c) the P24T microprocessors. The '486 and P24T use external 32-bit connections, and the Pentium has a full 64 bits.

### 3.3 V PROCESSOR

From the early days of *TTL digital electronics*, an operating voltage of 5 V has been standard. Many of the microprocessors used in PCs have developed from this early technology, and have also used 5 V. From as early as 1992, a version of the 386 microprocessor was available that operated from 3.3 V. Today's modern higher speed Pentiums and 486DX4 series microprocessors are all available with operating voltages of 3.3 V.

Why? There is nothing particularly special about either of these voltages, other than it must be appreciated that reducing the voltage used by logic circuits results in a substantial reduction in power consumption and generated heat. Halving the supply voltage will reduce the power consumption by three quarters. An operating voltage of 3.3 V is chosen because the level remains compatible with existing 5 V circuitry, but significantly reduces the power consumption and heat generated within the microprocessor.

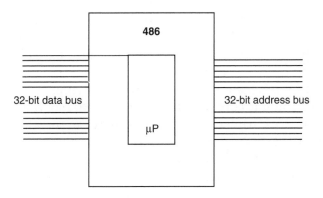

**Fig. 3.8(a)**  Data connections for the 80486

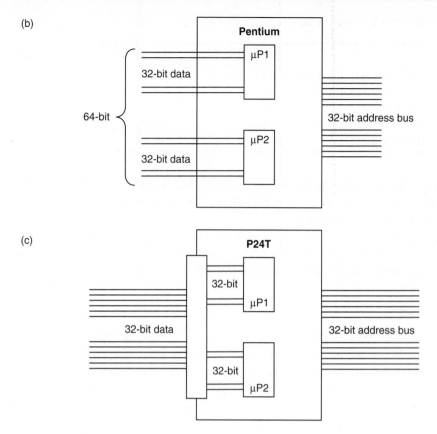

**Fig. 3.8**   Data connections for (b) the Pentium; (c) the P24T

## Clone manufacturers

Although Intel microprocessors have been discussed in the main, it must be appreciated that there are manufacturers worldwide producing what can best be described as 'clone microprocessors'. Manufacturers such as Cyrix, AMD, NexGen and IBM themselves may produce either direct equivalents, or in some cases, processors designed to improve on the original. Many of these processors may only be compatible at software level; as they have different pin arrangements they may not be socket compatible. Typical examples are IBM's 'Blue Lightning' and Cyrix's 5x86 (M1) microprocessor chips.

The Blue Lightning is comparable with Intel's 80486, but has 16 Kb of cache and an internal clock tripler, and operates at 3.3 V. The chip is designed to fit into the standard '386DX socket.

The Cx 5x86-100 provides an example that operates at 100 MHz internally with a 32-bit data bus and is designed to be used in 33 MHz 64-bit system boards. The L1 cache is 16 Kb, and recommendations are that the chip be used with 256 Kb of external L2 cache. The two integer units are pipelined with seven stages:

pre-fetch, decode 1, decode 2, address calculation 1, address calculation 2, execute and write-back. The pre-fetch stage involves gathering and evaluating the instructions, and the two decode stages determine the length of the instructions and then decode. The address calculations determine which of the processor's registers are to be used and access memory, with the actual arithmetic or logical processes performed at the execute stage. Finally, the write-back stage returns the resultant data through buffers to cache and memory.

## Developments to date

Table 3.3(a) and (b) provides a summary of the major improvements made to date in the 80x86 family and similar devices. The table also includes basic details for recently released sixth-generation processors, which are discussed in the following pages.

## Future developments

Talk of future developments is aimed at the recent official releases of sixth-generation computers. Considering the rate at which developments are leaping along, at the time of publication many of these systems will be in the shops, possibly at relatively realistic prices. A whole new language is being introduced to support these new systems and their up-to-date-and-beyond microprocessors, much of which goes further than the purpose of this book. For those who cannot wait, a brief discussion of Intel's Pentium Pro and AMD's NexGen Nx686 is included.

*PENTIUM PRO*

Processor manufacturers seem intent on breaking new ground, and the Pentium Pro (P6) is no exception. The next generation in a line of developments in the '386, '486, Pentium family, the Pentium Pro introduces several new features aimed at improving performance. Operating speeds are likely to be 200 MHz, and with a 64-bit data bus, 8 Kb L1 data cache, 8 Kb L1 instruction cache, and 256 Kb L2 burst-mode pipelined cache, the Pentium Pro is an impressive device.

The block diagram in Fig. 3.9 is a simplified representation of the internal workings of the Pentium Pro, and is included as an introduction to some of the latest developments. Many of the blocks service functions that have already been discussed. The bus interface unit, L1 and L2 cache, FPU, and execute and fetch/decode units all perform tasks relevant to their titles. A new concept, the retirement unit, is a term used to describe the process of committing the results of executed operations to their original program order.

**Table 3.3(a)** Microprocessor development: data and memory

| | Data bus width (bits) | | Address bus | Accessible |
| --- | --- | --- | --- | --- |
| | Internal | External | width (bits) | Memory |
| 80286 | 16 | 16 | 24 | 16 Mb |
| 80386SX | 32 | 16 | 24 | 16 Mb |
| 80386DX | 32 | 32 | 32 | 4 Gb |
| 80486SX | 32 | 32 | 32 | 4 Gb |
| 80486DX | 32 | 32 | 32 | 4 Gb |
| 80486DX2 | 32 | 32 | 32 | 4 Gb |
| 80486DX4 | 32 | 32 | 32 | 4 Gb |
| Blue Lightning | 32 | 32 | 32 | 4 Gb |
| Cyrix 5x86 (M1) | 64 | 32 | 32 | 4 Gb |
| NexGen 586 | 64 | 64 | 32 | 4 Gb |
| Pentium | 64 | 64 | 32 | 4 Gb |
| P24T | 64 | 32 | 32 | 4 Gb |
| Pentium Pro | 64 | 64 | 32 | 4 Gb |
| Nx686 | 64 | 64 | 32 | 4 Gb |

**Table 3.3(b)** Microprocessor development: speed, FPU and cache

| | Clock speed (MHz) | | Internal | Integral | Internal |
| --- | --- | --- | --- | --- | --- |
| Microprocessor | External | Internal | multiplier | FPU | cache |
| 80286 | 12–20 | 12–20 | 1× | No | No |
| 80386SX | 16–33 | 16–33 | 1× | No | No |
| 80386DX | 20–40 | 20–40 | 1× | No | No |
| 80486SX | 16–66 | 16–66 | 1× | No | 8 Kb |
| 80486DX | 33 | 33 | 1× | Yes | 8 Kb |
| 80486DX2-50 | 25 | 50 | 2× | Yes | 8 Kb |
| 80486DX2-66 | 33 | 66 | 2× | Yes | 8 Kb |
| 80486DX4-75 | 25 | 75 | 3× | Yes | 8 Kb |
| 80486DX4-100 | 33 | 100 | 3× | Yes | 8 Kb |
| Blue Lightning | 33 | 100 | 3× | No | 16 Kb |
| Cyrix 5x86 (M1) | 33 | 100 | 3× | Yes | 16 Kb[a] |
| NexGen 586 | 33 | 100 | 3× | No | 32 Kb |
| Pentium[b] | 50–66 | 60–166 | 1–2.5× | Yes | 16 Kb |
| P24T | 33 | 33 | 1× | Yes | 16 Kb |
| Pentium Pro | 50–66 | 150–200 | Up to 3× | Yes | L1 16 Kb |
| | | | | | L2 256 Kb |
| Nx686 | –[c] | –[c] | –[c] | Yes | 48 Kb |

[a]Also has additional 256 byte instruction cache.
[b]See comparison of Pentiums in Table 3.1.
[c]Not known at the time of writing.

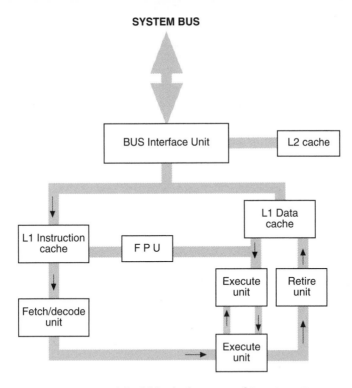

**Fig. 3.9** Simplified block diagram of Pentium Pro

*NX 686*

The Nx686 from AMD/NexGen increases the number of execution units to seven: the load unit, store unit, two integer units, FPU, multimedia unit and branch unit, all of which are controlled by an instruction control unit. Figure 3.10 outlines the basic layout of these new features.

The approach used for internal cache is slightly different to that adopted for the Pentium Pro. L1 cache consists of 32 Kb for data and 16 Kb for instruction. L2 cache is entirely external, but the processor is designed to work with up to 2 Mb.

## Summary

This chapter has introduced some of the terminology associated with the micro-processor, not only in the use of the words, but also by looking at block diagrams that explain internal operations. It is not essential to have a great technical understanding of the workings of the processor but some appreciation will enhance your overall perception of the system. The following self-assessment questions will give an indication of the depth of understanding that you should now have achieved.

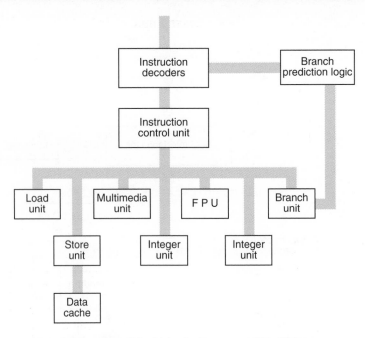

**Fig. 3.10** Simplified block diagram of Nx686

## Self-assessment questions

1. Sketch a simplified block diagram for a basic microprocessor.

2. Outline the basic features of the following microprocessors:
   (a) 80386SX          (c) Pentium
   (b) 80486DX          (d) Cx586-100

3. Give brief explanations for the following terms:
   (a) L1 cache         (d) Burst mode
   (b) L2 cache         (e) Pin grid array package
   (c) Pipelining       (f) Virtual-8086 mode

## Answers

Relevant reading material is indicated below by the page number corresponding to the question.

1. page 41

2. (a) pages 49, 58      (c) pages 51, 58
   (b) pages 51, 58      (d) pages 56, 58

3. (a) page 43           (d) page 47
   (b) page 43           (e) page 44
   (c) page 47           (f) page 46

# Basic jargon

*Arithmetic and logic unit (ALU).* The ALU undertakes the decision making by processing data and instructions.

*Burst mode.* Burst mode of operation transfers data in a single burst without intervention from the microprocessor.

*Bus cycle pipelining.* Allows a second process cycle to start before the first has finished.

*Clock cycle.* The duration in which the clock pulse goes through a complete cycle of 'ON' and 'OFF'.

*Clocked logic.* A process of using timing pulses to step through instructions within a program.

*Core frequency.* The internal operating frequency of a chip.

*Execution unit.* A modern term used to describe an area of a chip which is designed to process data and instructions, e.g. the ALU.

*First-level (L1) cache.* Cache internal to the microprocessor used for specific tasks, e.g. data and instruction cache.

*Operating modes.* A term used to describe the different ways in which a microprocessor can function.

*Primary cache.* Cache housed inside a microprocessor.

*Second-level (L2) cache.* Cache used for general-purpose functions. Originally external to the microprocessor but becoming more popular internally.

*Secondary cache.* See *Second-level cache*.

*Surface mount technology.* A manufacturing process used in the electronics industry that mounts electronic components such as chips directly on to the surface of the circuit board, i.e. not by inserting component leads through holes in the board.

*TTL digital electronics.* A type of electronics that uses only two specific levels of 0 V and 5 V to represent data as 'OFF' or 'ON'.

*Write-back caching.* A method by which data are transferred into cache without accessing memory.

*Write-through cache.* A method by which data are transferred to memory each time the processor writes to cache.

# 4
# The expansion bus

## Expansion bus architecture

As system speeds advanced from the 8 MHz processors used in very early PCs, some peripherals connected to the system could not cope, and needed to operate at the original slower speeds. A bus standard was adopted that included the original system bus made up from the data, address and control buses collectively, but with the addition of an expansion bus that could operate independently. Figure 4.1 illustrates this arrangement using a 32-bit 33 MHz microprocessor as an example.

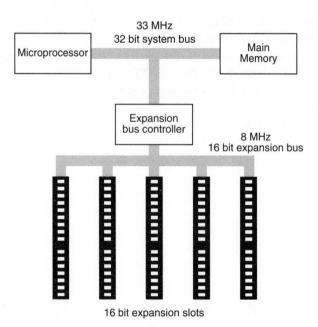

**Fig. 4.1**  Traditional bus architecture

The system bus provides a data path with width and speed comparable with the processor, i.e. 32-bit and 33 MHz for a 486SX/33, and has traditionally been reserved for use with the processor, cache, and main memory. The expansion bus provides physical connections between the processor bus and peripherals at a much lower speed, and in many systems with a reduced bus width, i.e. 16-bit at 8 MHz.

Looking at the diagram in Fig. 4.1, it becomes apparent that as processors have increased in speed and bus widths, this method of expanding the system creates a bottleneck between the system bus and expansion bus. In the example given, the data width is reduced to half, and the speed by about a quarter, with a significant effect on reducing the system's overall performance.

*EARLY DEVELOPMENTS*

The original PC/XT expansion used an 8-bit data bus offered through a 62-pin socket called an expansion *slot*. In an 8-bit system this was referred to as an *8-bit slot*. The 62 pins were needed for data, addressing, control and power supplies.

With the introduction of the AT, using faster microprocessors with greater capacity, the need for an improved expansion bus continued to grow. IBM provided a solution by adding another connector in line with the older 8-bit slot for a further 8 bits, and some additional features. Together these two connectors formed a 16-bit slot. This AT expansion bus is now commonly referred to as the industry standard architecture (ISA) bus, and formed the basis for future developments. Some early 80386-based systems still provided at least two 8-bit slots alongside the new 16-bit standard. This was due to the existence of some 8-bit adaptor cards that would not physically fit into the new slots.

The 80386-based systems increased the demand for an expansion bus that enabled the full use of the chip's 32-bit power. Several manufacturers produced their own 32-bit standards, resulting in a range of connectors used for the expansion slots. Two examples gaining most prominence were the micro channel architecture (MCA) standard used by IBM in their later PS/2 models, and the extended industry standard architecture (EISA) designed as an alternative to MCA.

Both the MCA and EISA bus standards have 32-bit bus widths and support bus mastering, can operate at higher speeds, and provide software set-up of adaptor cards. Although bus mastering and software set-up are possible with these standards, many MCA- and EISA-compatible cards have made little use of the potential.

The MCA used a range of connectors for the expansion slots dependent on the features offered, but were never designed to be compatible with the ISA standard. IBM's patent and copyright constraints imposed on the cloning of the MCA expansion bus were the main influences in several manufacturers seeking an alternative 32-bit version.

That alternative proved to be the EISA standard. Having similar technical features to MCA, it was compatible with ISA to the extent that the expansion slots provided would also take 16-bit ISA adaptor cards. This *backward compatibility* provided the user with a cost-effective method of upgrading to an EISA system board, by using some of the existing 16-bit adaptor cards.

Continued improvements in microprocessor speed and video performance increased the pressure for even faster and more powerful expansion bus standards, leading to a development called the local bus.

*LOCAL BUS*

Local bus architecture uses a technique involving an additional bus operating at speeds near to that of the microprocessor, and provides a similar bus width. The local bus concept is illustrated in Fig. 4.2.

Rapid transfer of large amounts of data is made possible by providing a short-cut between the microprocessor and additional devices. The expansion bus controller communicates with the local bus as if it were another peripheral. Using a local bus, high-performance graphic cards and IDE disk drives can bypass the bottleneck of the traditional expansion bus and operate much more quickly.

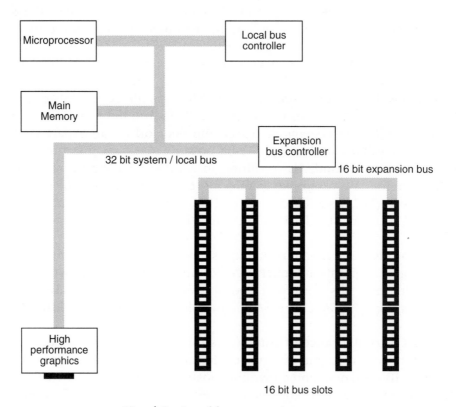

**Fig. 4.2**   Local bus expansion

The standard expansion bus is still available to slower peripherals such as printers and fax/modems.

*VESA LOCAL BUS*

Announced in 1992, acceptance of the Video Electronics Standards Association (VESA) local bus by industry was almost instant. The specification was developed by VESA, and is also referred to as the VL bus or simply VLB. The standardized connector used is an extension to existing 16-bit ISA slots, and once again provided backward compatibility in enabling the use of earlier 16-bit cards.

A note of warning for anyone working with VESA local bus adaptor cards. Although the VESA specification is standard, not all manufacturers have adopted the standard in the same way. Before installing VESA adaptors you should ensure that the system board, the card and connected devices are compatible with one another.

At the time of writing, VESA's latest local bus standard is soon to be released. The Vesa LB Version 2.0 is designed with a 64-bit width suitable for use with Pentium-based systems, and permits an increase in the number of expansion slots possible in a circuit. The specification includes backward compatibility allowing cards from the original VLB to work with the new slots and vice versa.

*PCI LOCAL BUS*

Intel's own version of the local bus has progressed to the current 32/64-bit peripheral component interconnect (PCI) bus, now gaining tremendous popularity in modern systems – the 64-bit architecture is ideally suited to the Pentium-based systems. The PCI bus is a high-performance local bus supporting multiple peripherals. The basic principles of PCI are illustrated in Fig. 4.3, which shows the relationships between system bus, traditional expansion bus, and PCI local bus.

An independent bridge between the microprocessor and peripheral devices acts as a controller between buses, maintaining high speed and data capacity. The traditional expansion bus is still retained to serve the needs of slower peripheral devices such as printers and modems.

An entirely different connector is used for the PCI expansion slot, making earlier ISA-based cards incompatible, and possibly contributing towards a slower initial uptake of the standard.

PCI has four fundamental differences.

❑ PCI can run at a higher speed, currently up to 66 MHz.
❑ PCI supports bus mastering.
❑ PCI supports 'plug and play', a method for automatic set-up of adaptor cards using software (discussed later).
❑ The chips used for PCI also support ISA and EISA, so expansion slots for all can be included on the same system board.

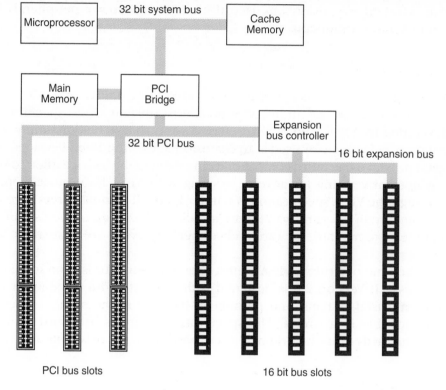

**Fig. 4.3** PCI local bus

*PLUG AND PLAY*

Plug and play (PnP) is not an expansion bus, it is not a 'hardware device', nor is it a 'piece of software', and 'it' cannot be purchased across the shop counter to upgrade your system. The term was introduced by Intel to describe a system that does not rely upon hardware set-up for PCI adaptor cards (i.e. *DIP switches* and *jumpers*). A PCI configuration program records system information relating to the set-up of adaptor cards or devices that can be accessed via software instead of removing the system cover every time to gain access. The concept is to make upgrading with the addition of adaptor cards and peripherals easier in the future, removing many of the associated configuration difficulties.

*PCMCIA BUS*

Both manufacturers and users have become familiar with the expandability of PC systems based on expansion slots. If the principle of expansion capability was to be adopted in laptop and notebook computers, an appropriate standard had to be developed. The Personal Computer Memory Card International Association (PCMCIA) established a specification for credit card-sized memory expansion cards, which has been extended to include a variety of card types. The cards range from Type I (1), used for memory, through to Type IV (4), used for a range of functions including removable hard disk drives. All are designed to slide into small slots on laptop and notebook systems.

*UNIVERSAL SERIAL BUS*

The universal serial bus (USB) is one of the latest developments likely to hit the home markets in late 1996. The planned specification builds on the developments of the plug and play concept by providing the opportunity for easy connection of external peripherals to the PC.

The driving force behind the USB is from the increased demands made on the peripheral ports for a range of applications such as connection to telephone equipment. The number of possible peripheral connections on current systems is usually two or three via the serial ports on the back of the PC. USB increases the maximum number possible to 126, if you can afford them, all of which will be of a plug and play standard.

The USB has three basic elements to the system: the host (the PC), the hub (a central distribution connection), and the functions (the connected peripherals).

Figure 4.4 shows how every conceivable peripheral might be connected through a single connector from your PC either (a) in a *daisy chain* with one device after another, or (b) using a hub arrangement.

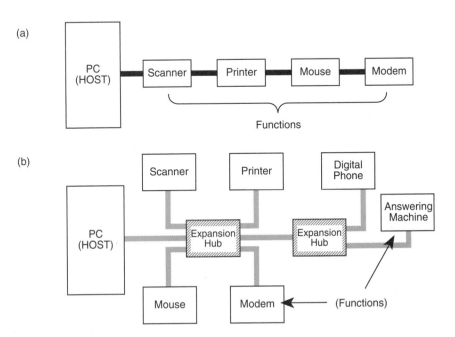

**Fig. 4.4**   (a) Daisy chain arrangement using USB; (b) hub arrangement using USB

## BUS MASTERING

Traditionally, the microprocessor controlled virtually everything in the system. In the very early stages of computer development this was not a problem since, if not in direct control, there was little else for the processor to do. With advancements in new technology and improved speeds of operation, a point was reached when the demands on the processor increased significantly and methods had to be developed to free up some of the processor's time for other tasks. One such development was the bus master.

A bus master is a device that, in addition to the microprocessor, can take over the system bus to control the flow of data, e.g. between hard and floppy disk drives, freeing the microprocessor to complete other tasks. This improves the flow of data, making it faster than direct memory access (DMA), but it can only reach full potential when used with multitasking operating systems.

## COMPARISON OF BUS ARCHITECTURES

A summary comparison of the different bus standards is provided in Table 4.1. The first three columns are fairly self-explanatory, with the first column indicating the bus standard, and the second the width of the data bus. The maximum speed is intended as a guide, and can vary between manufacturers. The transfer rate is a term used as a measure of performance and is an indication of the amount of data that can be transferred along the bus in one second. The units used are megabytes per second (Mb/s) where 1 Mb/s is equivalent to 1 048 576 bytes per second. The final two columns show the bus standards which support bus mastering and PnP.

**Table 4.1** Comparison of bus standards

| Bus standard | Data width (bits) | Maximum speed (MHz) | Typical transfer rate (Mb/s) | Bus mastering | PnP |
|---|---|---|---|---|---|
| 16-bit ISA | 16 | 8 | 8 | ✗ | ✗ |
| EISA | 32 | 8 | 33 | ✔ | ✗ |
| MCA | 32 | 20 | 80 | ✔ | ✗ |
| VLB | 32 | 33 | 132 | ✔ | ✗ |
| VLB Ver.2 | 64 | 50 | 400 | ✔ | ✔ |
| PCI 32 bit | 32 | 66 | 264 | ✔ | ✔ |
| PCI 64 bit | 64 | 66 | 528 | ✔ | ✔ |

✔, present; ✗, absent.

# Expansion slots

A modern PC system can be equipped with a variety of expansion bus slots. These depend primarily upon the width of the data bus and the bus architecture used.

Most of the expansion slots provide identical signals – the data bus, address bus, and control signals, with some limited exceptions depending on the specific needs of the bus architecture. Remember that the purpose of the expansion slots is to provide an easy method for expanding the system by adding or changing adaptor cards. However, note that on many compatible systems it is standard procedure to include the basic necessities on the system board. These might include video output, mouse connector, and parallel/serial ports, and the number of expansion slots available is sometimes limited. This often complicates matters when considering upgrading the system.

There are five basic types of expansion bus slots common to modern PC systems, plus the PCMCIA expansion cards used for laptops and notebooks:

- industry standard architecture (ISA) bus
- extended industry standard architecture (EISA) bus
- Video Electronics Standards Association (VESA) local bus
- micro channel architecture (MCA) bus
- peripheral component interconnect (PCI) bus
- Personal Computer Memory Card International Association (PCMCIA).

*ISA BUS SLOT*

The original 8-bit XT expansion bus used a single 62-pin connector, making use of 31 pins down either side of an adaptor card edge-connector. The 16-bit ISA bus added a 36-way in-line connector, increasing the total number of connections to 98 as shown in Fig. 4.5.

*EISA BUS SLOT*

EISA is a 32-bit expansion bus, designed by manufacturers seeking an alternative to the MCA standard, which provides backward compatibility with the ISA 8 and 16-bit bus adaptor cards. This is achieved by adding 90 additional connections without increasing the physical size of the ISA slot. Note that 100 pin positions are available for additional connections, but 10 of these are replaced by 'keys' to ensure correct insertion (see Fig. 4.6b). The EISA slot, mounted on the system board, looks similar to that used for the 16-bit ISA, but uses smaller contacts and contains a second row of connections deeper in the slot.

This can be seen more clearly by comparing the diagram of an ISA card edge-connector in Fig. 4.6(a) with the corresponding edge-connector of the EISA card shown in Fig. 4.6(b).

The lowest level contacts (EISA) connect to the extended 32-bit bus, whilst the upper level contacts (ISA) provide the 8 and 16-bit connections. The access

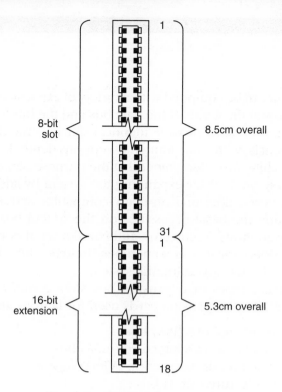

**Fig. 4.5** ISA bus slot connectors

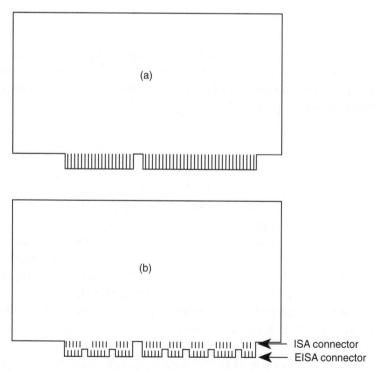

**Fig. 4.6** (a) ISA card edge-connector; (b) EISA card edge-connector

keys prevent an ISA card from being inserted far enough into the slot to make contact with the lower connections of the EISA extended bus.

*MCA BUS SLOT*

There are several different arrangements for the MCA slots involved in IBM's PS/2 style of PC: the 16-bit slot, the 32-bit slot and a range of extensions for video and memory. The diagrams in Fig. 4.7 illustrate the connectors used for a sample of the possible arrangements. The connector pins are smaller than those found on ISA or EISA slots, hence adaptors are not interchangeable.

The main MCA slot shown in Fig. 4.7(a) is divided into two sections, one handing 8-bit operations (pins 1–45), and the other 16-bit operations (pins

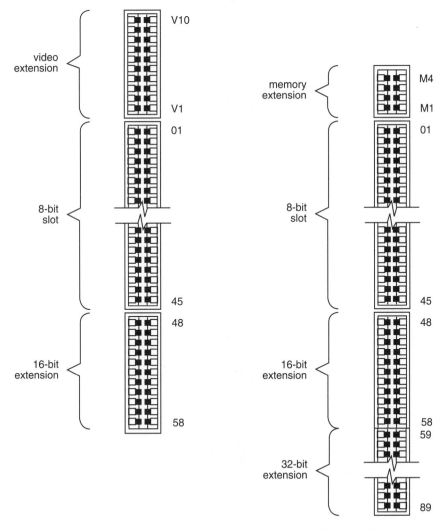

**Fig. 4.7** MCA bus slot: (a) 16-bit with video extensions; (b) 32-bit with memory extensions

48–58). It can be seen that pins 46 and 47 are not used. These are removed and form a key preventing incorrect insertion of the card. The standard 16-bit slot can be enhanced with the optional addition of a video-extension connector (pins V1–V10) which is used for fast exchange of video signals.

MCA systems based on a '386 or higher microprocessor have several 32-bit designs to take full advantage of the processor's capabilities. The example shown in Fig. 4.7(b) has an additional memory section (pins M1–M4) with a further bus expansion up to 32-bit (pins 59–89).

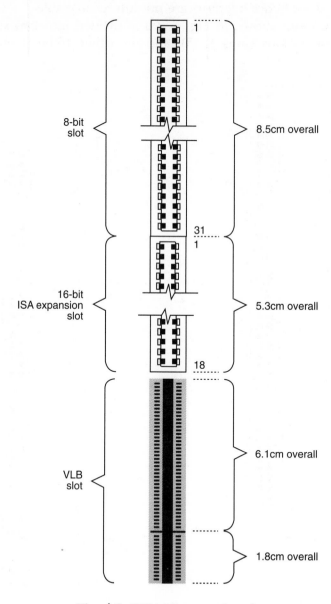

**Fig. 4.8**  VESA LB expansion slot

*VESA LOCAL BUS SLOT*

Physically, the VESA slot is an extension to the 16-bit ISA slot with an additional connector, similar in appearance to the MCA connector, positioned immediately in front of the existing 16-bit ISA slot, as shown in Fig. 4.8. This single connector is usually referred to as the VESA LB slot, and the original as the ISA slot. The extra VESA LB slot has 58 pin positions down either side with two on each side used for a key. This produces an additional 112 contacts (116 – 4). The arrangement enables the slot to be used with either VLB devices using the VESA slot or 16-bit devices using the ISA slot.

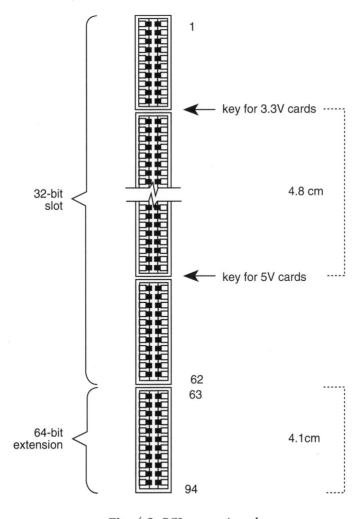

**Fig. 4.9** PCI expansion slot

*PCI LOCAL BUS SLOT*

The PCI expansion slot uses a connector more likened to that used for MCA than the ISA version. The arrangement is made more complicated by the range of different types available. The PCI adaptor card comes in 32 or 64-bit versions, each operating at either 5 V or 3.3 V.

Pins 1–62 are used for 16-bit functions, and pins 63–94 for the 64-bit extension. The identification between voltage types is achieved using pins 50 and 51 as a key in 5 V cards, and pins 12 and 13 as a key in 3.3 V cards. This may sound confusing, but careful examination of the diagrams in Fig. 4.9 should help you with identification.

*PCMCIA CARDS*

The range of PCMCIA cards available is increasing steadily. A summary of the different types includes the following:

Type I     The original standard used for memory expansion cards, and designed with a 3.3 mm thick card.

Type II    Supporting virtually any type of expansion device, the cards used are 5 mm thick. By design, the type I cards can be used in type II slots.

Type III   This type is intended for use mainly with removable hard disk drives, with slots that are 10.5 mm thick.

Type IV   Intended also for use with hard disk drives, the type IV slot is larger.

The simplified diagram in Fig. 4.10 illustrates a typical PCMCIA card.

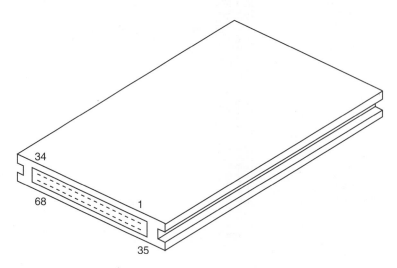

**Fig. 4.10** Typical PCMCIA adaptor card

# Adaptor card identification

There was a time when virtually every added function for the PC used an adaptor card, hence the large number of adaptor slots on early systems. Consider the functions that might be needed. Internally a card for hard disk, floppy disk, and CD-ROM drives, and externally cards for video, game port, serial and parallel ports (mouse and printer). On modern systems many functions are often provided on a single multi-I/O card that serves hard and floppy disk drives, serial and parallel ports, and probably even a game port. Although many manufacturers are including functions such as disk drive connections on the system board, and some compatible manufacturers put all of the main functions on the system board, the number of different plugs and sockets can create confusion. The following notes will help when an unknown adaptor card is presented, or when trying to identify the rear connectors on an unlabelled system:

When establishing the function of an adaptor, there are three parts of the card to take into consideration:

- the external connectors that can clearly be seen at the rear of the system unit and are often mounted on the rear plate of the card
- the internal connectors mounted on the card circuit board
- the edge connectors at the bottom of the board that depend upon the type of bus used.

Figure 4.11 shows a typical adaptor card and possible layout including external and internal connectors.

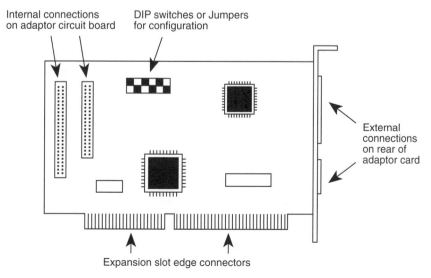

**Fig. 4.11** Layout of typical adaptor card

*ADAPTOR EXTERNAL CONNECTORS*

A common connector type used on the rear of adaptor cards is the D shell, so called because of its similarity in shape to the capital letter D. It comes as a plug, with pins for contacts, or as a socket, and is available in 9, 15, 25 or 37 contact variations. A nine-pin D plug is often referred to as a 'male DB9', and a 25-contact socket as a 'female DB25'. Other types of connectors are used for specialist functions and care should be taken not to confuse them. Examples are provided in Fig. 4.12 and Appendix F.

*ADAPTOR INTERNAL CONNECTORS*

Connectors used internally on the circuit boards tend to be less varied. Other than special connectors used by some compatible manufacturers the main connectors likely to be found inside are for the floppy disk, hard disk, and CD-ROM drives. These usually have a linear pin-cushion arrangement with the number of pins depending upon the device connected. Figure 4.13(a) shows a common combination of 34-pin floppy disk drive and 40-pin IDE hard disk drive, with Fig. 4.13(b) showing the older ST506 20-pin data and 34-pin control connectors.

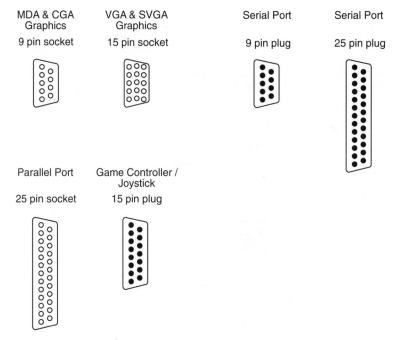

**Fig. 4.12** Adaptor card external connectors

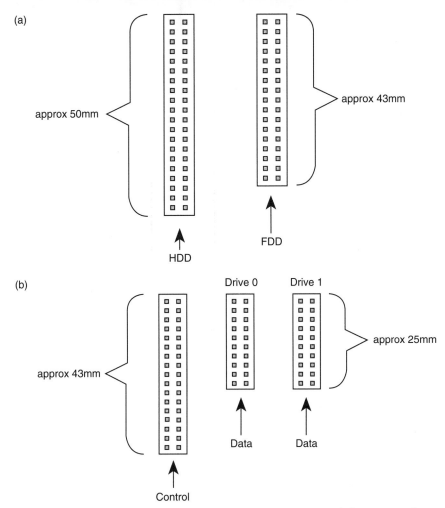

**Fig. 4.13** (a) FDD and IDE HDD connectors; (b) ST506 data/control connectors

*EXPANSION BUS CONNECTORS*

The sockets used for the expansion bus have been described in some detail earlier in this chapter, and more specific information is provided in the Appendix D. The diagrams in Fig. 4.14 (a–c on page 78, d on page 79, and e on page 80) can be used to help in identifying the expansion bus for which a card has been designed.

*ADAPTOR COMPATIBILITY*

It should now be apparent that most of the adaptor cards used for different expansion bus standards are not compatible or interchangeable. Table 4.2 provides a summary of the adaptor cards and the expansion slots with which they are compatible. It should be noted that even where a 16-bit card can physically be used in a 32 or 64-bit slot, the card will still only operate at 16 bits.

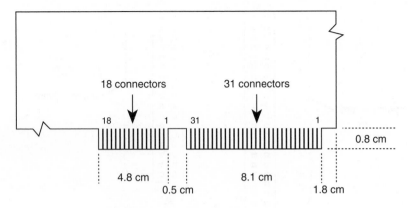

**Fig. 4.14(a)** ISA adaptor card

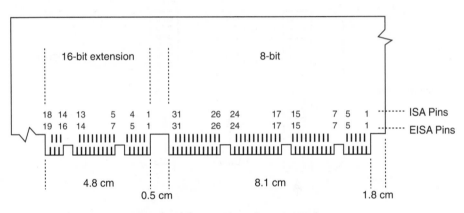

**Fig. 4.14(b)** EISA adaptor card

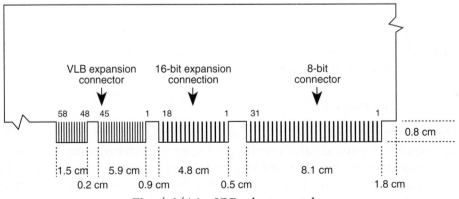

**Fig. 4.14(c)** VLB adaptor card

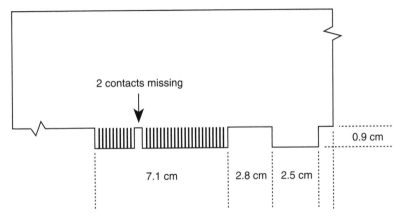

**Fig. 4.14(d)**   MCA adaptor card

**Table 4.2**  Expansion card compatibility

| | Slot | | | | | | | |
| | ISA | EISA | VLB[a] | VLB[a] | MCA | MCA | PCI | PCI |
| Card | 16-bit | 32-bit | 32-bit | 64-bit | 16-bit | 32-bit | 32-bit | 64-bit |
|---|---|---|---|---|---|---|---|---|
| ISA 16 bit | ✔ | ✔ | ✔ | ✔ | ✗ | ✗ | ✗ | ✗ |
| EISA | ✗ | ✔ | ✗ | ✗ | ✗ | ✗ | ✗ | ✗ |
| VLB 32 bit | ✗ | ✗ | ✔ | ✔ | ✗ | ✗ | ✗ | ✗ |
| VLB 64 bit | ✗ | ✗ | ✔[b] | ✔ | ✗ | ✗ | ✗ | ✗ |
| MCA 16 bit | ✗ | ✗ | ✗ | ✗ | ✔ | ✔ | ✗ | ✗ |
| MCA 32bit | ✗ | ✗ | ✗ | ✗ | ✗ | ✔ | ✗ | ✗ |
| PCI 32 bit | ✗ | ✗ | ✗ | ✗ | ✗ | ✗ | ✔ | ✔ |
| PCI 64 bit | ✗ | ✗ | ✗ | ✗ | ✗ | ✗ | ✔[b] | ✔ |

[a]VLB refers to the combined ISA 8 and 16-bit slots with the VLB extension.
[b]When a 64-bit PCI or VLB card is used in a 32-bit slot, it will operate as a 32-bit card.
✔, compatible; ✗, not compatible.

## Summary

Developments in expansion bus architecture have been led by demand for many years. Motivated by the need for greater bus width and flexibility, modern systems have come a long way since the original 8-bit PC bus. This chapter has introduced these developments and some of the terminology necessary to understand bus operations and identify the different types of adaptors in a system. The questions ending the chapter, and the exercises in Chapter 8 will provide additional knowledge and understanding.

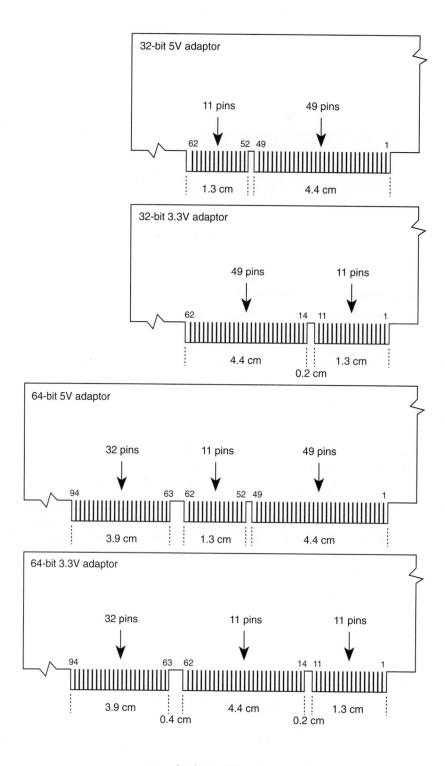

**Fig. 4.14(e)** PCI adaptor card

## Self-assessment questions

1. List the main characteristics of the following bus systems:
   (a) ISA 16-bit   (c) VESA LB
   (b) EISA         (d) PCI LB

2. What type of peripheral is most likely to be connected to the following adaptor connectors:
   (a) Male DB9 'plug' on back panel
   (b) Female DB25 'socket' on back panel
   (c) 40-pin linear pin connector on adaptor board?

3. What advantages will Plug and Play have over other systems?

## Answers

Relevant reading material is indicated below by the page number corresponding to the question.

1. (a) page 63      (c) page 65
   (b) page 63      (d) page 65

2. (a) page 76
   (b) page 76
   (c) page 77

3. page 66

## Basic jargon

*Backward compatibility.* A term used to describe the compatibility of a system or device with older systems or devices.

*8-Bit slot.* An adaptor slot that provides access to the 8-bit expansion bus.

*Daisy chain.* The connection of several devices following one another to a cable.

*DIP switch.* A small switch mounted on a circuit board usually used to select configuration settings in a similar way to a jumper.

*Jumper.* A two-pin connector used to join together pins to act as a switch. Jumpers are used to select configuration settings on system boards, drives and adaptors.

*Slot.* The connector into which adaptors are plugged, and which provides access to the system or expansion bus.

# 5
# Memory

Memory is essential to the operation of a working computer. With the latest advances in design and reductions in cost, memory chips in your PC are a possible option for upgrade. This is likely to involve main memory dynamic RAM (DRAM), although in some cases it might include the addition of static RAM (SRAM) cache.

## DRAM and SRAM

Different techniques are used to manufacture memory, with a range of advantages and disadvantages. The two main types in use are DRAM and SRAM.

DRAM comes in a variety of shapes and sizes, and provides the main memory in a system. Each memory cell stores data using the charge on a capacitance, which can be thought of as like charging a battery, but over a much shorter period of time (nanoseconds rather than hours). In the same way that batteries lose their charge due to leakage currents, so does the capacitor. In DRAM this charge needs to be topped up at regular intervals, i.e. refreshed. This *refresh* process is the reason behind the term 'dynamic'.

SRAM works in a very different way. It is manufactured from transistor circuitry in the form of *latches*, the contents of which remain fixed until written to, or until the power is removed. Without the need for refreshing, associated electronic circuitry tends to be simplified.

Both DRAM and SRAM are suited to construction in integrated circuit form. DRAM chips have larger cell densities and lower power consumption, but slower access times. SRAM is faster but has lower cell densities. As a result SRAM chips are much more expensive than DRAM, and hence they are used for special memory devices such as cache memory.

### ORGANIZATION OF MEMORY CELLS

In memory devices the basic storage element consists of a single cell that has the capacity to store 1 bit of information, and each cell needs to be identified individually. Large capacity memory devices found in computers arrange the cells in a two-dimensional array or grid, consisting of rows and columns. Each cell can be identified uniquely by its row and column address. The diagram in Fig. 5.1 shows how the shaded cell can be identified by the address 'C6' – row C, column 6.

For a real memory device to function correctly, there are additional requirements.

❏ It is likely that there will be more than a single chip, therefore selection of a particular chip becomes necessary – *chip select*.
❏ A bus connection for the transfer of data.
❏ A method of indicating whether the data are being written to or read from the chip – *read/write select*.
❏ A decoder to convert the coded addresses for row and column into a suitable format for the chip to handle – row and column *address decoders*.
❏ Signals to indicate whether a row or a column is being accessed. These two signals are called the *row address strobe (RAS)* and *column address strobe (CAS)*, respectively.

Some of these requirements are shown in Fig. 5.2. This diagram is a simplified version of the actual circuitry and is provided for interest to those who wish to have a little more understanding of the terminology used.

*SRAM CACHE*

When used to store instructions or data currently in use by the microprocessor, memory must have access times comparable with, and be as close as possible

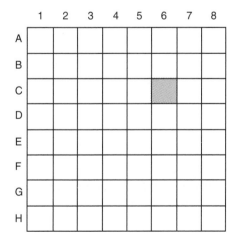

**Fig. 5.1**   Two-dimensional array

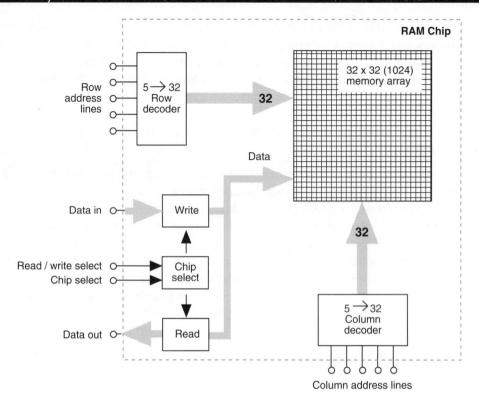

**Fig. 5.2** Organization of memory cells

to the processor. If not, the processor would have to wait, resulting in the whole system slowing down. SRAM is used extensively for cache memory, which compensates for some of the bottlenecks resulting from the microprocessor trying to access slower devices. Modern systems have the capacity for using two types of cache, primary and secondary.

Primary cache memory is placed within the microprocessor on chips like the '486 series. Typically, the '486 provides 8 Kb of very fast RAM, and the Pentium, 16 Kb. As prices fall, and processor and software needs increase, the demand for faster memory continues to grow. Historically, secondary cache is mounted on the system board and is becoming very popular as a means of boosting performance. Consisting of up to 1 Mb of very fast SRAM, these are usually identified as one or more long dual in-line (DIL) chips in close proximity to the microprocessor.

The general rule is that fast memory is rare and expensive, whilst slower memory is common and relatively cheap. For a system to have large amounts of very fast main memory would be too costly. A compromise is achieved by using fast main memory DRAM at realistic cost, faster cache SRAM on the system board, and even faster memory in the processor itself, consisting of registers and cache.

*MEMORY HIERARCHY*

From the discussion of registers, primary and secondary cache, static and dynamic memory we have a memory hierarchy with varying access times.

At the top of the hierarchy are the processor registers, which are accessed at a similar speed to the processor. These are followed closely by the primary cache, which is accessed sufficiently quickly not to cause the processor any problems. The primary cache, when used for dedicated purposes, is often referred to as first-level cache (L1). The next level in this hierarchy is the secondary cache, which is used for general-purpose storage and is also referred to as second-level cache (L2). Although secondary cache has always been located on the system board, some manufacturers are now including second-level cache on the microprocessor chip. Towards the bottom of the hierarchy are the large amounts of main memory DRAM, relatively slow but fast enough to run general program code and store data. Finally, there are the mass storage devices such as disks and CD-ROM, which are to all intents and purposes memory devices with potentially huge capacities but much slower access times. Typical relationships between speed, location and cost are shown in Table 5.1.

A modern system may consist of 8 or 16 Mb of main memory DRAM, 256 Kb of secondary cache SRAM, and 8 or 16 Kb of primary cache SRAM inside the processor.

*EDO MEMORY*

Extended data out (EDO) memory is a new type of high-performance memory that can perform twice as quickly as conventional DRAM and is available in standard single in-line memory module (SIMM) packaging. When main memory DRAM operates, irrespective of how it is packaged, there is a very short period between data outputs when the memory is effectively idle. This is as a result of the way in which the CAS controls the data output. A fuller explanation is not

**Table 5.1** Memory comparison

| Type | Access time | Function | Location | Cost |
|---|---|---|---|---|
| Register | Comparable to processor | Storage for processor | Internal | Expensive |
| Primary cache L1 | <25 ns | Dedicated storage | Internal | Less expensive |
| Secondary cache L2 | 25 ns | General storage | System board (also internal) | Less expensive |
| Main memory | 70–100 ns | Main storage for system | System board | Relatively inexpensive |

possible without entering into the realms of page-mode cycles and other such complex activities. Be content with knowing that modern system boards using the latest in-chip design such as the Triton PCI chipset work at their best when using EDO DRAM.

## Packaging

There are three main packages used in the range of memory devices produced for PCs: the DIL, single in-line package (SIP) and SIMM. An example of each is given in the diagrams in Fig. 5.3.

DIL chips are single devices, with two lines of pins either side of a plastic or ceramic body. Used extensively for SRAM in secondary cache memory, and BIOS ROM, these are available in a range of configurations from 8-pin to 40-pin. They may be soldered directly on to the board or mounted in sockets. Although used in older systems for DRAM main memory, in modern PCs the devices have been replaced by a more modular system.

The SIMM is a sub-assembly consisting of DRAM chips surface mounted on a small circuit board with connectors along the edge, as shown in Fig. 5.3(b). These modules plug directly into the system board using special sockets. This is currently the most popular form of main memory RAM in modern PCs, due in the main to the flexibility that this offers.

The SIP is similar to the SIMM except that the edge connections are replaced by a single row of pins, as shown in Fig. 5.3(c). This is sometimes referred to as a single in-line pin package (SIPP).

Although XT and some early AT systems used DIL chips for main memory, this practice is no longer followed. The range of DIL chips used and the organiza-

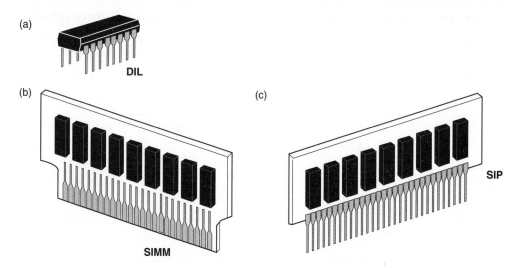

**Fig. 5.3** Memory devices: (a) DIL; (b) SIMM; (c) SIP

tion of these chips on system boards have been discussed in many text books and magazines in the past, at a time when it was appropriate. It is unlikely that you will need to replace multiple DIL DRAM chips in the modern PC, hence I spend no time discussing the procedures involved, but will concentrate on more relevant issues relating to the use of SIMMs as main memory devices.

*SIMM*

If you have seen any memory device from a modern PC then it is likely to have been the SIMM. The most popular structure is currently the 30-pin module, with three or nine surface-mounted chips, available in 256 Kb, 1 Mb, 4 Mb, 8 Mb, and 16 Mb capacities. In systems with data bus widths of 32 or even 64 bits, there is a need for memory modules with greater capacity. This is achieved using 72-pin SIMMs with individual capacities ranging from 1 to 64 Mb.

These small memory modules are mounted vertically in special sockets on the system board. This provides the user with an easy way of introducing large amounts of main memory into a standard system board. Chip manufacturers have standardized the use of SIMMs to some degree, but it is still very important when replacing or adding memory to ensure that the correct type is used. There are three main parameters, other than physical construction, that may vary from chip to chip – capacity (the number of bits), organization of the bits, and speed (access time).

Consider a single 1 Mbit chip. It could be organized as $1 M \times 1$ bit, $256 K \times 4$ bit, or $128 K \times 8$ bit. The '1 M', '256 K' and '128 K' indicate the number of addresses, and the '1 bit', '4 bit' and '8 bit' the number of bits stored at each address. All produce a 1 Mbit chip. This is important in understanding the arrangement of chips used on SIMMs which consist of several chips similar to those described.

If we stop to consider that the smallest data bus used in a PC is 8 bits wide, and that the larger bus sizes use multiples of 8 bits, this means that memory has to be organized in such a way as to provide 8 bits for every memory address. In order to do this, designers use combinations of chips as outlined in the example below.

The 30-pin SIMM is produced in slightly different formats with either nine chips or three chips. Figure 5.4 shows a typical nine-chip, 30-pin SIMM (9-bit). Each chip stores 1 bit for each address; eight chips are used for data, and the extra one for a *parity check*. This *parity bit* enables the system to perform an error-checking function, and to detect transient errors automatically. These are temporary errors that might result from a *spike* on the mains supply or other interference. The 30-pin SIMM is also available as an 8-bit device providing no facilities for parity checking.

The three-chip SIMM is still a 9-bit device in which two chips each store 4 bits for each memory address, and the third chip is used for parity checking and control. This arrangement is illustrated in Fig. 5.5.

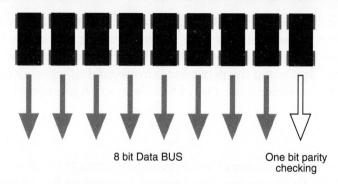

8 bit Data BUS                     One bit parity
                                   checking

**Fig. 5.4**   Organization of a nine-chip, 30-pin SIMM (9-bit)

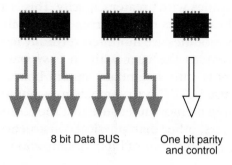

8 bit Data BUS              One bit parity
                            and control

**Fig. 5.5**   Organization of a three-chip, 30-pin SIMM (9-bit)

The standard 72-pin SIMM shown in Fig. 5.6 caters for the larger bus sizes used by modern microprocessors. It adopts a similar arrangement to the 30-bit version, and can deliver either a 16-bit or a full 32-bit bus width. The 72-pin SIMM is available in 36-bit and 32-bit versions. The 36-bit SIMM use 32 bits for data and 4 bits for parity checking, whilst the 32-bit version has no facilities for parity checking. In addition, some standards for 72-pin SIMMs include connections that allow your system to determine the speed of SIMM installed, which is then used to optimize performance automatically.

Table 5.2 provides a summary of the main types of SIMMs that are currently available.

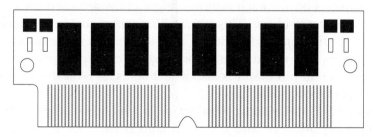

**Fig. 5.6**  A 72-pin SIMM

**Table 5.2** Summary of available SIMMs

| SIMM type | No. of chips | Bus width (bits) | Parity |
|---|---|---|---|
| 30-pin 9-bit | 9 | 8 | ✔ |
| 30-pin 8-bit | 8 | 8 | ✗ |
| 30-pin 9-bit | 3 | 8 | ✔ |
| 30-pin 8-bit | 3 | 8 | ✗ |
| 72-pin 36-bit | N/A | 32/64 | ✔ |
| 72-pin 32-bit | N/A | 32/64 | ✗ |

*MEMORY BANKS*

The memory requirements of a system are linked to the bus width of the microprocessor. The 16-bit processor shown in Fig. 5.7(a) will need to access 16-bits for data and two parity bits; assuming 30-pin modules are used, a bank of two SIMMs is necessary. When used with a 32-bit processor, the minimum number of 30-pin SIMM modules needed is four – each SIMM will handle 8 bits. This arrangement is illustrated in Fig. 5.7(b).

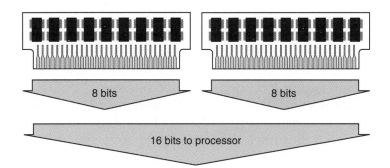

**Fig. 5.7(a)** The use of 30-pin SIMMs with a 16-bit microprocessor

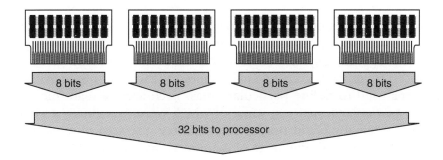

**Fig. 5.7(b)** The use of 30-pin SIMMs with a 32-bit microprocessor

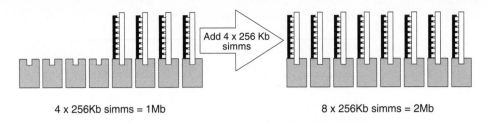

4 x 256Kb simms = 1Mb                    8 x 256Kb simms = 2Mb

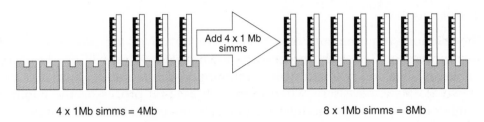

4 x 1Mb simms = 4Mb                      8 x 1Mb simms = 8Mb

**Fig. 5.8**  Combinations of SIMMs

It is important to note that if using 256 Kb SIMM modules, only 512 Kb of memory will be available in the first example, and 1 Mb in the second. This is insufficient for use with modern software, and has led to the rise in popularity of larger capacity SIMMs. This also highlights the point that SIMMs need to be added in banks of two or four, depending on bus size.

The arrangement of SIMM sockets on a system board varies, but often there are four or eight sockets. This provides flexibility in possible combinations of modules. Figure 5.8 illustrates the total capacity of a system using a range of different SIMM combinations.

## Memory map

Historical developments in PC memory are based on overcoming the limitations of the original 8086 microprocessor, and limits to the main memory recognized by the disk operating system (DOS). This has resulted in a range of techniques introduced to improve access to main memory, each technique bringing with it new terms used to define particular areas. Each area of main memory can be used for particular functions, some of which were introduced to make use of areas that originally could not be accessed, e.g. the area of memory from 640 Kb to 1 Mb. In general, the areas of main memory are classified as base, upper, high, extended and expanded. This structure is best represented graphically in the form of a memory map, as shown in Fig. 5.9.

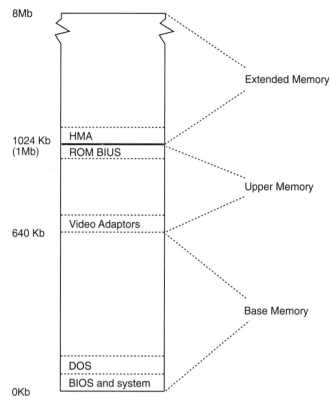

**Fig. 5.9** Typical memory map

For use with modern software, 1 Mb of main memory is unacceptable. The entry level at the time of writing is 8 Mb, with 16 Mb quickly becoming a popular option. The memory map in Fig. 5.9 also illustrates how the memory in a modern PC is extended beyond the 1 Mb barrier.

*BASE MEMORY*

The area between 0 and 640 Kb is the base memory or *conventional memory*. The area is used mainly for software applications, and is the absolute minimum requirement for DOS software applications. A small part of base memory is used by DOS to operate. The need to free up as much base memory as possible for software applications has resulted in manufacturers producing methods of using the upper and extended areas of memory.

*UPPER MEMORY*

Ranging from 640 Kb to 1024 Kb (1 Mb), the *upper memory area* is reserved for use by peripherals and device drivers – the software needed by hardware to function correctly. Any unused sections are called *upper memory blocks*, which in 80386 systems and later can be used for running device drivers and memory-resident programs. This is divided into specific areas for use by video adaptor, ROM BIOS, and program code and data for the system's installed device drivers.

*EXTENDED MEMORY (XMS)*

The memory area extending beyond 1 Mb is called extended memory, and to be of use it requires special extended memory manager software. Windows and Windows-based applications will not operate without extended memory, and the recommended minimum needed with entry-level systems is currently 7 Mb (plus 1 Mb base memory = 8 Mb total).

*HIGH MEMORY AREA*

The first 64 Kb of extended memory is given a special name: high memory area (HMA). DOS is usually installed in the HMA, leaving more conventional memory available for application programs.

*EXPANDED MEMORY (EMS)*

This is a term used in earlier systems, and refers to physical memory added beyond 1 Mb, but which had to be accessed as if it existed between 0 and 1 Mb. Systems developed after the 80286 have the capacity to access physical memory beyond 1 Mb, and use faster extended memory provision.

Installed on an expansion board, often using an adaptor card, expanded memory needed a special expanded memory manager. This manager provided access to a limited amount of expanded memory, 64 Kb at a time, and was therefore slower than when using extended memory.

Some application programs have used, and need expanded memory to operate. Both DOS and Windows can simulate expanded memory but modern software is now written for use with extended memory.

## Summary

Memory can be identified by its construction (DRAM and SRAM), use (main and cache memory), and classification (base, upper, etc.). Memory plays a major role in the development of PCs, and recent years have seen the basic PC progress to include 16 Kb primary cache, 256 Kb secondary cache, and at least 8 Mb of main memory. These developments have encouraged the production of new packaging such as the SIMM, which enables easier repair and upgrade of memory.

## Self-assessment questions

1. Explain the following terms:
   (a) SIMM
   (b) memory map
   (c) parity check
   (d) upper memory block

2. Explain the main differences between:
   (a) primary cache and secondary cache
   (b) DRAM and SRAM
   (c) base memory and extended memory
   (d) a nine-chip and three-chip 30-pin SIMM

## Answers

Relevant reading material is indicated below by the page number corresponding to the question.

1. (a)  page 87     (c)  page 87
   (b)  page 90     (d)  pages 91, 92

2. (a)  pages 84, 85     (c)  page 91
   (b)  page 82          (d)  page 97

## Basic jargon

*Address decoder*. Converts coded memory addresses into a format suitable for a chip to handle.
*Address strobe*. A signal used to indicate access to and produce data output from memory.
*Base memory*. The first 640 Kb of memory. Also called conventional memory.
*Chip select*. A connection used to activate the chip.
*Column address strobe (CAS)*. An address strobe controlling columns.
*Conventional memory*. The first 640 Kb of memory. Also called base memory.
*Expanded memory*. Physical memory above 1 Mb used in older systems, accessed as if it were conventional memory.
*Extended memory*. The memory area extending beyond 1 Mb.
*High memory area*. The first 64 Kb of extended memory.
*Latch*. An electronic device that can be switched from one state to another, i.e. ON or OFF, 5 V or 0 V. Used in memory devices, one state of the latch can be used to represent cell content.
*Parity bit*. A single bit added to the data used to identify errors.

*Parity check.* An error-checking function used to identify when an error occurs in reading data.

*Primary cache.* Cache memory contained within the microprocessor chip.

*Read/write select.* A connection to a chip that indicates whether data are to be written or read.

*Refresh.* A process used to maintain the contents of dynamic RAM by topping up the charge on memory cells.

*Row address strobe (RAS).* An address strobe controlling rows.

*Secondary cache.* Cache memory external to the microprocessor.

*Spike.* A mains spike is a large voltage pulse of very short duration caused by some form of interference in the mains supply.

*Upper memory area.* The memory area from 640 Kb to 1 Mb.

*Upper memory block.* Small areas of the upper memory used to run device drivers and memory-resident programs.

# 6
# System configuration

In order for your system to boot, it needs to be supplied with some basic information. 'What hardware it has' and 'what it's supposed to do' are a good start.

The 'what hardware' will include information about number and types of floppy/hard disk drives, the amount of memory, and type of display. This initial information makes use of a set-up program and CMOS RAM which are used to record basic system details. Physical configuration of adaptor cards and added peripherals is needed to prevent conflict, and this is achieved on all but the very latest PCs using jumpers and switches.

The 'what to do' may include details on how memory is to be allocated, or how a particular application package is to function. This type of information is provided by the user with software configuration files such as CONFIG.SYS and AUTOEXEC.BAT.

The importance of recording this information accurately and storing it safely cannot be stated too clearly. You will at some time either intentionally or accidentally erase configuration data or alter jumper settings, which will result in your PC being 'down' – not just a little under the weather, but totally unbootable. It is essential that you are in a position to be able to put this right, and that includes having accurate information to hand. Take this warning seriously and use the documentation provided in Appendix B, or something similar, to record all configuration information for your system.

## AT set-up

The original IBM PC used two banks of eight DIP switches for configuration, one bank to indicate the amount of memory installed, and the other for details of disk drives, video display and coprocessor. The only configuration DIP switch you are likely to find on an AT-based PC (early systems) is mounted on the system board in the corner near to the power supply and keyboard connectors. This DIP switch is used to select the primary display type, either monochrome or colour.

In all modern PCs, system configuration data together with day and time information are held in a special CMOS RAM that can be accessed using the AT set-up program or purpose-designed software.

*CMOS RAM*

The system set-up data and date/time information are contained in a 64-byte section of special CMOS RAM commonly referred to as the CMOS chip. It is unlikely that you will ever want to access these data directly (set-up does it for you), but it is interesting to see how such an apparently detailed amount of information is contained in a relatively small space. Table 6.1 shows how the data are distributed through the 64 bytes of memory. The bottom 14 bytes are used by the real-time clock (RTC; Table 6.1a), and the remainder for the storage of set-up data (Table 6.1b). Some of the terminology will be unfamiliar to you, but

**Table 6.1** CMOS contents

(a) Real-time clock

| Offset address (bytes) | Contents/function |
|---|---|
| 00 | Seconds |
| 01 | Second alarm |
| 02 | Minutes |
| 03 | Minute alarm |
| 04 | Hours |
| 05 | Hour alarm |
| 06 | Day of the week |
| 07 | Date of the month |
| 08 | Month |
| 09 | Year |
| 10 | Register |
| 11 | Register |
| 12 | Register |
| 13 | Register |

(b) Typical CMOS contents

| Offset address (bytes) | Contents/function |
|---|---|
| 00–13 | Real-time clock data |
| 14 | Diagnostic status byte |
| 15 | Shutdown status byte |
| 16 | Floppy disk type (A and B) |
| 17 | Reserved |
| 18 | Hard disk type (C and D) |
| 19 | Reserved |
| 20 | Equipment byte |
| 21 | Base memory, low byte |
| 22 | Base memory, high byte |
| 23 | Extended memory, low byte |
| 24 | Extended memory, high byte |
| 25 | Hard disk C: extended byte |
| 26 | Hard disk D: extended byte |
| 27–45 | Reserved |
| 46 | CMOS checksum |
| 48 | Actual extended memory, low byte |
| 49 | Actual extended memory, high byte |
| 50 | Date century byte |
| 51 | POST information flags |
| 52–63 | Reserved |

there is no need for concern since the point of access to these data will be through the set-up program. Later systems have increased the size of the CMOS RAM to 128 bytes to hold data for other system features.

As with all RAM, the CMOS is volatile, and needs to be maintained by a battery so that set-up information is not lost when the system is switched off. Some systems use rechargeable Nicad batteries, whilst others use non-rechargeable lithium batteries, either of which may be soldered directly on to the system board or connected by a short lead. Modern systems use a combined memory and battery housed together in the chip. Manufacturers' quotes for the life-span of a battery vary between 3 and 10 years. Your only guarantee is that the battery back-up for your CMOS RAM should be OK for several years. If the CMOS battery fails, or is inadvertently disconnected, data will become invalid, and will need to be restored to original settings. This may cause problems unless original settings are recorded in system documentation.

# Running set-up

In systems such as those employing MCA or EISA expansion buses, a set-up program is provided on floppy disk. In most other systems the set-up program is built into the ROM BIOS. The first of these methods is discussed in many earlier publications, hence the following explanations will be based only upon the popular built-in set-up. These built-in programs can be activated in one of several ways.

❏ By pressing a key (often 'Esc' or 'Del') when prompted by the BIOS. Usually this is immediately after the memory test at power-on, or following the configuration report.
❏ By using a special key sequence pressing several keys together, e.g. Control-Alt-Esc or Control-Alt-S.

If the displayed information is incorrect, it can be changed using a combination of cursor movement keys, Page Up/Down keys or the Tab key. Set-up programs when activated often display a warning message noting that incorrect set-up may prevent the system from operating. This acts as a good reminder to document all information before making any changes.

Most set-up programs offer stages of access at different levels. A typical program might consist of a main menu screen, providing access to *standard set-up* and *advanced set-up* menus.

*SET-UP MAIN MENU*

The main menu often provides several utilities associated with configuration, disk drives and passwords, together with access to higher levels of configuration. Table 6.2 provides a summary of the most frequently encountered terms used and a brief explanation of each.

**Table 6.2** Set-up main menu

| Term used | Function |
| --- | --- |
| Standard CMOS | Activates the standard set-up menu |
| Advanced CMOS | Activates the advanced set-up menu |
| Auto configuration | Enables the use of default values for CMOS provided by the manufacturer |
| Password | Enables the use of a password to prevent unauthorized access to set-up – difficult if the password is forgotten |
| Hard disk utilities | A range of utilities for formatting and changing interleaving for hard disk drive – these are not for the beginner<br>Also 'auto-detect', which will automatically determine the CMOS details for the installed IDE hard disk drive – IDE only |
| Write to CMOS | Several ways of exiting set-up will include options to 'write to CMOS' (save changes), or 'not write to CMOS' (changes not saved) |

*STANDARD CMOS SET-UP*

Standard set-up is probably the menu most likely to be used, providing access to date/time, disk drives and displays. A typical standard CMOS display is shown in Fig. 6.1 and a blanked out copy is provided for recording purposes in Appendix B.

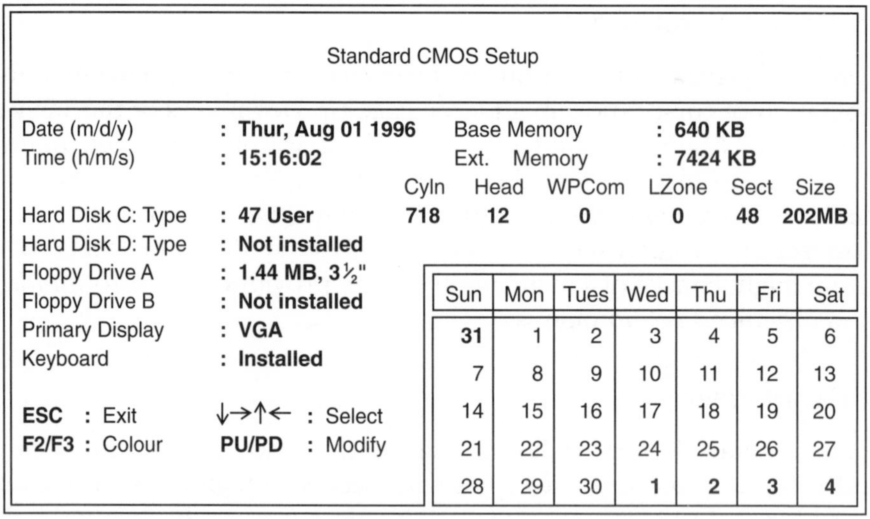

**Fig. 6.1** Standard CMOS Set-up display

Information relating to base and extended memory is entered automatically by the system, and all other entries can be modified by the user if incorrect. This is possible using the cursor movement keys to select the relevant section, then pressing the Page Up or Page Down key to move through the available options. The Escape key is pressed to exit set-up.

Some of the sections are easily answered by entering the date, time, and type of drive for A: and B:. Other sections are a little more difficult and need further explanation.

The hard disk type section allows the entry of essential details for hard disk drives to be used as C: or D: drives. The details include number of cylinders, heads and sectors, *write precompression*, and *landing zone*, with an automatic entry for size. This will apparently offer 47 different options, the first 46 of which are already defined for popular drives, and type 47 for user-definable drive types, allowing you to enter details directly under each heading. When installing IDE drives, the auto-detect utility available from the main menu will enter details automatically into the CMOS set-up.

The primary display type is used to indicate the type of monitor connected to the main video display.

The keyboard section is used to indicate the installation of a keyboard, or more importantly if a keyboard is NOT installed. During the boot process the keyboard is tested. Normally, if a keyboard is not present an error message is displayed on the screen and the boot process is terminated. If the option 'not installed' is selected for the keyboard section this error will not be generated, and the system will continue to boot. Although not immediately apparent, there are some instances when a PC might be used without a keyboard installed, and this facility is useful.

*ADVANCED CMOS SET-UP*

The many features available with advanced set-up vary with both the BIOS and the chipset. Changing the options for most of these features will produce a substantial effect on the operation of your PC which will not necessarily be to your advantage. Do not tinker with these options unless you are absolutely sure of the effect!

There are exceptions. Two features that you may at some time wish to modify, which will not cause serious problems, are listed in Table 6.3 together with basic explanations and recommended settings.

*RECOVERY*

In order to protect you from yourself, or from others, many manufacturers provide you with get-out-of-trouble recovery options: a jumper that when connected resets the CMOS contents to the original factory settings (see system board manual), or a default selection from the set-up main menu as discussed

**Table 6.3** Advanced set-up boot sequence

| Feature | Function | Normal setting |
|---|---|---|
| System boot sequence | Allows you to select the order of disk drives from which the system boots, either hard disk (C:) first, or floppy disk (A:) first.<br>Selecting the boot from hard disk speeds up the boot process. | C:; A: |
| Floppy drive seek at boot | Enables or disables the ability of the system to boot from floppy. | Enabled |

in Table 6.2. PCs not offering either option can usually be reset by disconnecting the back-up battery for a short time.

Once the system has recovered sufficiently to enable the boot process and allow access to set-up, your previously recorded configuration information can be re-entered. This task is made even easier using one of the commercially available software packages that allows you to save your configuration data to floppy disk and reinstall whenever necessary.

A final note with regard to the hard disk drive settings. If the information for your hard disk drive is lost and the system will not even acknowledge its existence, you must boot from the floppy disk drive using a system disk (see notes in Chapter 7 – Fault-finding Techniques).

## Physical configuration

Physical configuration can be thought of as the connections and settings for all of the hardware that have not already been covered. These will include jumper and DIP switch positions on the system board and any adaptor cards, connections from the system board to other devices and the front panel, and even the types and slot position of adaptor cards. The jumper and switch positions on adaptor cards have particular significance because these would normally relate to parameters that can cause problems when adding or upgrading adaptors. The most common purposes for jumpers and switches are to select specific values for each card for interrupt request (IRQ), direct memory access (DMA) channel, and input/output (I/O) address, none of which should create problems when plug and play becomes standard.

*IRQ*

An interrupt is the method used by peripheral devices (disk drives, printer, mouse, etc.) to gain the attention of the microprocessor. The request tells the processor that the peripheral requires something attending to, and the processor acknowledges this request, takes appropriate action, and then returns to its original task.

Unfortunately, if two or more devices share the same IRQ line and are active at the same time, conflict will occur. The processor will not be able to distinguish between the devices and will not be able to determine the correct action. For this reason each device or adaptor card is assigned to an IRQ line, or channel. When the device needs to interrupt the processor, it sends a signal to the interrupt controller down its designated IRQ line on the expansion bus. The interrupt controller can then identify which device requires attention. Ideally, each device would have its own IRQ line with no two devices ever sharing. In practice this is often difficult except in the most basic of systems and careful juggling is the only answer.

The original 8-bit ISA system had only eight interrupt lines, whereas the 16-bit ISA, EISA, MCA and later versions all have 16 – a necessary number in modern systems using a whole range of additional devices. Each IRQ is allocated an identifying number, 0–15, which is also used to indicate the level of priority, level IRQ0 having the highest priority, and level IRQ15 the lowest.

In order to provide 16 levels of interrupt, two 8259A interrupt controllers (or their equivalent in an integrated support chip) are used, each handling eight individual interrupts. Controller number one handles IRQs 0–7, and controller number two IRQs 8–15. The first controller has direct access to the system, but the second provides interrupts indirectly through the first, using IRQ2. This arrangement is illustrated more clearly in Fig. 6.2.

It might help to appreciate that the IRQ lines are physical electrical connections, some of which are made available on the connections to the expansion bus slots, e.g. IRQ5 is made available on pin B23 of the 8-bit section of the ISA expansion slot (see Appendix D for expansion slot connectors). The more astute of you may now be aware that this information can help in identifying the IRQ line used by an adaptor card for which technical information is not available,

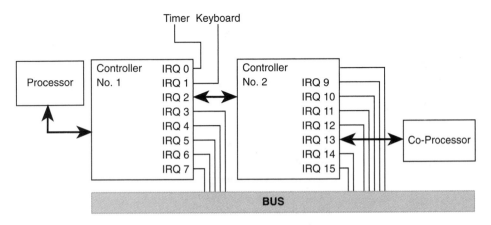

**Fig. 6.2** Arrangement for interrupt controllers

e.g. if you have an adaptor card and the only IRQ line connected to the edge connector with a copper track is pin B21, then this card must use IRQ7 (check Appendix D for connections). On modern adaptor cards facilities are normally provided using jumpers to select different IRQ lines, but the choice is usually limited.

Some interrupts are reserved for internal operations, and are therefore not available to the expansion bus. The availability of interrupts, allocation to bus slots, and typical assignments are listed in Table 6.4.

When installing adaptor cards and peripheral devices it is important to consider several basic points.

❏ Keep an accurate record of all installed devices and any modifications.
❏ Any interrupt that is listed as in use by a device or adaptor which is not installed will be available, e.g. if the system does not have a parallel port LPT2, then IRQ5 is available.
❏ Any secondary device or adaptor must use a different interrupt to the original if they are likely to be accessed at the same time, e.g. hard disk controllers usually use IRQ14, and the suggested IRQ for a secondary controller is IRQ15. The relevance of this can be clarified by checking with Table 6.5.
❏ The ROM BIOS may only support certain interrupts for particular applications. If this is the case, any additional controllers must have on-board BIOS.

**Table 6.4** Typical system interrupts

| IRQ | Typical assignment | Bus slot |
|-----|-------------------|----------|
| 0 | System timer | ✗ |
| 1 | Keyboard controller | ✗ |
| 2 | Second IRQ controller | ✗ |
| 3 | Serial port 2 (COM2) | ✔ |
| 4 | Serial port 1 (COM1) | ✔ |
| 5 | Parallel port 2 (LPT2) | ✔ |
| 6 | Floppy disk controller | ✔ |
| 7 | Parallel port 1 (LPT1) | ✔ |
| 8 | Real-time clock | ✗ |
| 9 | Available | ✔ |
| 10 | Available | ✔ |
| 11 | Available | ✔ |
| 12 | System board mouse port | ✔ |
| 13 | FPU/maths coprocessor | ✗ |
| 14 | Hard disk controller | ✔ |
| 15 | Available | ✔ |

**Table 6.5** Typical IRQs and I/O addresses

| Device/function | IRQ No. | Bus | Pin No. | I/O port address |
|---|---|---|---|---|
| System timer | 0 | ✗ | N/A | 040–05F |
| K/B controller | 1 | ✗ | N/A | 060/064 |
| Second IRQ controller | 2 | ✗ | N/A | 0A0–0BF |
| Serial port COM2 | 3 | 8-bit | B25 | 2F8–2FF |
| Serial port COM4 | 3 | 8-bit | B25 | 2E8 |
| Serial port COM1 | 4 | 8-bit | B24 | 3F8–3FF |
| Serial port COM3 | 4 | 8-bit | B24 | 3E8 |
| Parallel port LPT2 | 5 | 8-bit | B23 | 278– 27F |
| Floppy disk controller | 6 | 8-bit | B22 | 3F0–3F7 |
| Parallel port LPT1 | 7 | 8-bit | B21 | 378–37F |
| RTC | 8 | ✗ | N/A | 070–07F |
| Redirected IRQ2 | 9 | 8-bit | B 4 | |
| Available | 10 | 16-bit | D 3 | |
| Available | 11 | 16-bit | D 4 | |
| M/board mouse | 12 | 16-bit | D 5 | 061 |
| Coprocessor | 13 | ✗ | N/A | 0F8–0FF |
| Hard disk controller | 14 | 16-bit | D 7 | 1F0–1F8 |
| Available | 15 | 16-bit | D 6 | |

*DMA CHANNELS*

DMA is a technique allowing rapid transfer of data between peripherals and memory without intervention from the microprocessor. Each device or adaptor needing DMA is assigned a DMA channel which is used exclusively. In modern systems eight channels are available, DMA0–7, provided by two controllers in a similar arrangement to that used with IRQ lines. Access to all eight DMA channels is achieved using two 8237A controllers (or equivalent in an integrated support chip). Controller number one handles channels 0–3, and controller number two channels 4–7. The first controller has access via the second using DMA channel 4. As with IRQs, DMA channels are best not shared.

The original purpose of DMA in 8-bit systems was to provide high-speed data transfers for hard disk controllers. In modern 16-bit systems and higher, methods other than DMA are used, which produce even greater performance.

❑ Programmed input/output (PIO) whereby bytes of data are sent through I/O ports (DMA not required).
❑ Using bus master devices that override the DMA controller circuitry and effectively take over control of the bus. These bus masters must be assigned a DMA channel to operate. Bus mastering is discussed further in Chapter 4 – The Expansion Bus.

The basic points outlined when handling arrangements for IRQs, such as accurate records and availability, are equally important for DMA channels, although there is usually more flexibility.

*I/O PORT ADDRESSES*

Once an interrupt request has been raised, the microprocessor acknowledges the request and communicates with the interrupting device. In order to communicate, an address in memory is allocated to the device. This is a special address used solely for the device on that particular interrupt, and should not be shared with other devices.

The numbering system used to identify addresses is usually based on HEX, a numbering system that has 15 as a base rather than 10. In other words, the system can be used to count up to 15 using only a single character to represent each number. 0 to 9 are used as normal but then A, B, C, D, E, and F are used to represent 10, 11, 12, 13, 14, and 15, respectively. This accounts for the use of letters in many diagrams associated with memory and address allocations. If you are considering further investigation into these areas a basic understanding of HEX would prove useful.

## Summary

The main points covered in this chapter relate to the importance of obtaining and recording system configuration information, the most important being the data contained in the CMOS set-up. A record should be made of the CMOS set-up data, all installed devices and adaptor cards, their addresses and interrupts. New cards should be configured to use available interrupts only.

Exercises 2 and 3 in Chapter 8 help to identify and record this information on the System Documentation Form in Appendix B.

Interrupt assignments and their associated addresses are summarized in Table 6.5. The table also indicates their availability to the system bus, which bus and the corresponding expansion slot pin number.

## Self-assessment questions

1.  List typical IRQs, I/O addresses and expansion slot pin numbers for the following devices:
    (a)  printer connected to LPT1
    (b)  modem connected to COM2
    (c)  keyboard controller
    (d)  the floppy disk drive controller

2.  List the main functions for which you might use Standard CMOS set-up.

3.  What details are you likely to need to configure a new IDE hard disk drive?

# Answers

Relevant reading material is indicated below by the page number corresponding to the question.

1.  (a)  page 103      (c)  page 103
    (b)  page 103      (d)  page 103

2.  page 98

3.  page 99

# Basic jargon

*Advanced set-up.* A menu within the CMOS set-up program that enables access to advanced configuration data.

*Landing zone.* An inner cylinder on a hard disk drive at which the heads should be parked. This is achieved automatically on modern drives.

*Standard set-up.* The main menu from the CMOS set-up program which enables modification of essential configuration data.

*Write precompression.* A method of compensating for the smaller sectors towards the centre of a hard disk, improving data-write performance. This indicates the track at which write compensation begins.

# 7
# Fault-finding techniques

## First steps

Your PC is a combination of hardware and software that uses a very logical method of operation. It needs to know precisely where everything is, it needs to keep everything 'tidy' and ensure that all components are kept in step. When working on a PC you should take a tip from the expert (the PC itself!) and adopt similar principles. These can be characterized by a few basic rules.

❏ Know your PC; have a good basic understanding of what hardware it contains and how it works.
❏ Have a complete record of the CMOS set-up configuration details and important files, with back-ups. If possible back up your whole system.
❏ Have a usable set of installation disks for applications.
❏ Have a set of emergency diskettes (discussed later).
❏ Be methodical, approach the task with a clear mind, and in an orderly way.
❏ Give the problem some thought before diving in at the deep end.
❏ If in any doubt, **seek advice**.

### ORDER, ORDER!

Having gained an understanding of the PC, and having completed the documentation for your system, you can now consider investigating the world of troubleshooting. At this point I will remind you of an issue I raised in the Introduction to this book. If you or your employer have just purchased a Pentium Multimedia PC or similar, you are strongly advised not to tamper with a perfectly functional piece of equipment. If you want to experiment then obtain an older, cheaper system to work with, which will probably prove more rewarding anyhow – less stress for a start! Assuming that you now have in your possession a system in need of attention, the first process is that of diagnosis.

# Diagnostics

Before any fault can be repaired, a logical process needs to be followed in order to establish the reason for the fault. This is a process of diagnosis that involves careful assessment of the symptoms and any history leading up to the malfunction.

The types of diagnostics available to the PC user fall into three basic levels:

- power-on self-test (POST) procedure
- routine-user diagnostics
- advanced-user diagnostics and utilities.

*POST PROCEDURE*

Whenever the power is switched on, or the system rebooted, the BIOS automatically performs a series of self-tests referred to as POST. The system is tested in a specific order that may vary slightly from system to system, but the basic sequence includes the system board, ROM, display, memory and major peripherals. If POST discovers a problem, an error message is generated that may take the form of an audio code (series of beeps) and/or a visual code number displayed on the screen. Table 7.1 provides a much simplified summary for the sequence of tests performed by the POST in a Compaq '486 system. The table also provides basic details for some of the error messages produced by the BIOS if the test fails.

This list is not complete and serves only as an example. With some BIOSs there are more than 30 individual steps in addition to the ones listed, including

**Table 7.1**  POST summary

| Basic test | Audio error | Visual error |
|---|---|---|
| Microprocessor | None | 1xx |
| ROM BIOS | — • | 101 |
| Keyboard | None | 3xx |
| Memory up to 256 Kb | None | 2xx |
| Video adaptor | — • • | 5xx |
| DMA controllers | None | 113 |
| PIC | None | 104 |
| Memory above 256 Kb | None | 2xx |
| Floppy disk drive | Various | 6xx |
| Hard disk drive | Various | 17xx |
| Parallel port | • • | 4xx |

• , short bleep; — , long bleep; 'xx' indicates a number.

**Table 7.2** POST error codes

| Error code | Hardware |
|---|---|
| 1xx | Microprocessor (system board) |
| 2xx | Main memory |
| 3xx | Keyboard |
| 4xx | Parallel port |
| 5xx | Video display |
| 6xx | Floppy disk drive |
| 11xx | System board |
| 17xx | Hard disk drive |
| 24xx | EGS/VGA board |
| 86xx | Pointing device (mouse) |

initialization of peripherals, displaying BIOS information on the monitor, and a final beep to show that all is well (two beeps on some systems). You can see and hear this process to some extent by observing the system as it boots. *LEDs* will flash, drives will come to life for a short time, and beeps will be heard, all indicating that tests are underway.

Visual POST error codes generated by a typical BIOS are summarized in Table 7.2. The codes include only an overview, where 1xx is used to signify any number between 100 and 199, 4xx signifies a number between 400 and 499, and so on. The coding systems used can provide much more detailed information than that indicated in the table, but the errors described by such codes go into more detail than the theoretical depth intended in this book.

These codes will vary from one BIOS to another. A simple example includes the code 4xx, which in the table is used for printer adaptor, whereas it is used by IBM for monochrome video errors.

**Table 7.3** Routine-user diagnostic software

| Source | File name | Function |
|---|---|---|
| DOS | DIR | An internal command in COMMAND.COM |
| | CHKDSK | Checks the status of a disk |
| | MEM | Displays how memory is utilized |
| | MSD | Microsoft Diagnostics – displays detailed information about the system |
| Norton | SYSINFO | Displays detailed information about the system |

## ROUTINE-USER DIAGNOSTICS

I would define routine-user diagnostics as those software aids to troubleshooting that enable the regular user of a PC to access detailed information about the system and its operation. These consist of a wide range of programs, some of which will already be installed on your system, supplied by the manufacturer, or alternatively can be purchased from software vendors at an affordable price. Table 7.3 summarizes some of the software available including Microsoft programs provided with later versions of MS-DOS, and popular utilities from the Norton stable.

The list is not exhaustive and I recommend reading the DOS manuals and guides provided with your system, which you were always going to read when you had time.

## ADVANCED-USER DIAGNOSTICS AND UTILITIES

Many of the advanced diagnostic packages available go beyond what is considered to be purely diagnosis. Most also provide repair and recovery options. The advanced utilities listed in Table 7.4 are just a small example of the large range commercially available which provide more extensive procedures and are aimed at the level of the technician. This is the person who is usually called in

**Table 7.4** Advanced-user utilities

| Source | Menu or file name | Function |
|--------|-------------------|----------|
| DOS | FDISK | Configures a hard disk for use with DOS. Used to partition the disk before high-level formatting. |
| | FORMAT | Formats a disk for use with DOS. |
| | SYS | Creates a boot disk by copying hidden system files (MSDOS.SYS and IO.SYS) and the command interpreter (COMMAND.COM). |
| | DEFRAG | Reorganizes files on a disk to optimize performance. Not to be used when running Windows. |
| | UNFORMAT | Restores a disk that was erased using FORMAT. |
| | SCANDISK | Similar to CHKDSK, checks status of a disk. Do not use when running Windows unless you use the switch/check only, i.e. SCANDISK /CHECKONLY. |
| Micro2000 | Micro-Scope | Universal diagnostic software and test utilities. See later notes – Advanced diagnostic tools. |
| Norton | NDD | Norton Disk Doctor – automatically detects and corrects disk errors. |
| | DISKEDIT | View and edit contents of a disk. |
| | DISKTOOL | Utilities to make disks bootable and recoverable. |
| | SFORMAT | Safe format to format a disk safely without erasing data. |

when the going gets tough, but very often solves the problem with the simpler methods discussed earlier, and a little thought.

The tools used for advanced work can be divided into three main areas:

- service and maintenance manuals
- advanced diagnostic utilities
- hardware add-in devices.

Service manuals are a useful aid to the experienced technician in providing a vast amount of technical information, and often diagnostic tools. The information supplied, and usually the cost of purchase take the use of such manuals beyond the scope of this book.

Not all utilities available for advanced users are complex or expensive. Microsoft provide some fairly advanced utilities within MS-DOS. Table 7.4 provides a brief summary.

More powerful advanced utilities are available from a variety of third-party sources, but should be used with extreme caution (if at all!) by any user who is not familiar with the workings of a system or the operation of the utility. Many of the utilities available will not only permit the user access to the inner workings of a system, but also permit the user to make major changes to disk contents, system configuration and more. Modifications can be made to such an extent that the system may not recover. On a more positive note, advanced diagnostic software utilities can very often be invaluable when it comes to recovering from a major malfunction within the system, and are certainly very interesting to use.

Finally, the add-in devices include professional tools such as the POST card, an adaptor card that plugs into an expansion slot and tells you what is wrong. Examples of software packages and add-in devices are discussed in a later section – Advanced diagnostic tools.

*EMERGENCY DISKETTES*

When problems arise that prevent the hard disk drive from operating or the system from booting, it is useful to have a range of emergency diskettes available.

Typical examples of diagnostic software and utilities are illustrated in Table 7.5. Further explanation is provided in the following paragraphs. These include four disks which are basically a matter of producing copies from your hard disk drive. As you become more familiar with your system and commercially produced utilities you can build on your existing toolkit by adding some of the tools discussed later.

The system boot disk is the minimum needed to start up a system in the event of a hard disk drive failure. The CONFIG.SYS or AUTOEXEC.BAT files are deliberately excluded, so you would not expect the system to boot as normal, e.g. loading Windows. As you can see with the other emergency diskettes, all include these basic system files so you could boot from any one of them.

**Table 7.5** Emergency diskettes

| System boot disk | Replacement system disk |
|---|---|
| IO.SYS[a] | IO.SYS[a] |
| MSDOS.SYS[a] | MSDOS.SYS[a] |
| COMMAND.COM | COMMAND.COM |
| | CONFIG.SYS |
| | AUTOEXEC.BAT |

| Test disk 1 | Test disk 2 |
|---|---|
| IO.SYS[a] | IO.SYS[a] |
| MSDOS.SYS[a] | MSDOS.SYS[a] |
| COMMAND.COM | COMMAND.COM |
| CHKDSK.COM | FDISK.COM |
| MSD.EXE | FORMAT.COM |
| MEM | SYS.COM |
| DEFRAG | |

[a]These are hidden files and cannot be used with commands such as DIR. To copy these to a diskette you must use the SYS command. In systems that do not use MS-DOS the files may have different names, e.g. IBMBIO.COM and IBMDOS.COM.

The replacement system disk is intended to boot your system in the same way that it normally does. It therefore includes the same CONFIG.SYS and AUTOEXEC.BAT files as your hard disk drive. Please note that if your system loads Windows, this diskette cannot unless the hard disk drive is accessible. This disk is sometimes useful to check for corrupted boot files.

In addition to the standard system files, Test disk 1 provides some basic diagnostic tools useful for checking out the system and the hard disk drive. Test disk 2 provides a number of hard disk utilities that can be used to aid repair. These utilities could be combined on to one disk once you have gained some experience. The reason for keeping them separate at this stage is because of the disastrous effect that would result from accidentally using FORMAT on your hard disk.

# Advanced diagnostics tools

The average user is unlikely to need or be able to justify the cost of some of the advanced utilities available for PCs. However, if like me you become so engrossed in the workings of these mystical electronic instruments then you might just force yourself. There is nothing more rewarding then taking that old, 'dead' PC and bringing it back to life using the most up-to-date tools available. Just in case you are tempted, the following pages discuss some of the tools currently available.

*MICRO-SCOPE 6.0*

Not quite as you might first expect this is not a metal tube with lenses at either end. Produced by Micro 2000, Micro-Scope offers a suite of software diagnostic tools that can be used with virtually any PC independent of the operating system, i.e. will work with DOS, Windows, Unix, OS/2 and more. The outstanding features include accurate identification of IRQs, DMAs, addresses, and even chip manufacturers – extremely valuable when upgrading with additional adaptors. The extensive test facilities cover all hardware used in a typical PC, not only the microprocessor, memory, disk drives, etc., but also CD-ROM drives and sound cards. It can even be used to determine the condition of your CMOS back-up battery. To complement the package, Micro 2000 also offer excellent technical support to assist with troubleshooting problems.

*QAPLUS/FE*

A comprehensive set of software diagnostics produced by Diagsoft, QAPlus/FE can be used to test all of the standard hardware in your system, provides detailed information for all parts of the system, and offers a selection of powerful utilities for viewing and editing. Unlike some diagnostic packages, QAPlus/FE offers the capacity to run a system non-stop under full load, a process referred to as *burn-in*. This facility can be very useful when a fault is intermittent, since the test will record any problems that occur for later viewing.

*POST-PROBE*

Also produced by Micro 2000, the POST-probe is a universal POST card that plugs into an expansion bus slot and provides detailed information relating to fault finding. The card will work on any PC incorporating ISA, EISA, or MCA slots. Displays include a two-digit error code, and LED indicators for 5 V and 12 V supplies, clock, microprocessor/DMA operation. The error codes can be used in a similar way to those generated by the POST, but the benefit of using the POST-Probe is that it can be used on a 'dead' PC.

# The next step

Before attempting to make use of any diagnostic procedures, and especially before removing the cover, you should ask yourself a few basic questions.

❏ Have I checked the system installation? Is it switched on? Are all the leads connected? Are plug fuses OK?
❏ Is the CMOS configuration the same as the system documentation?
❏ Am I sure of the system configuration? Have there been any changes lately – new drives or adaptors?

❏ Has anyone done anything different with the system?

❏ Have I observed all of the symptoms? Have I confirmed other users' descriptions of symptoms?

❏ Have I made accurate notes and recorded symptoms for future reference?

*SAFETY FIRST*

❏ Make yourself aware of health and safety procedures and follow them.

❏ Always **switch off** before moving or replacing anything, including the cover, cables and internal units.

❏ Observe antistatic precautions when handling system components (see Appendix A).

*THE COVER REMOVED*

Once the cover is removed there are a few additional questions to be answered.

❏ Are all leads and connectors in place?

❏ Are there any signs of foreign bodies or contamination? It's surprising what coffee can do!

❏ Are all socketed chips seated correctly? If in doubt, ease out slightly and refit.

❏ Are components running at the correct temperature? Chips should feel hot to the touch, but not burning or cold.

Armed with appropriate answers but still a non-functional PC, it is time to test the system. It should be noted that in the case of a true hardware fault, software diagnostic utilities may be used to detect and analyse the problem, but cannot be used to effect a repair. Traditional fault-finding techniques should be used to establish the relevant component and a replacement obtained.

❏ Follow the troubleshooting flowcharts and advice given in the following pages. It is important to refer carefully to the advice given with each flowchart to check any peculiarities associated with the test.

❏ Always run diagnostics on a PC configured for normal use, unless there are specific reasons. This means that memory managers, disk caches, device drivers, etc., should not be installed into memory. Boot from a basic system disk without CONFIG.SYS and AUTOEXEC.BAT.

❏ If testing serial/parallel ports have the necessary *loop-back plugs*.

❏ Some tests take a long time. Before starting ensure that the system can be left unattended if necessary.

## Troubleshooting flowcharts

This section of the chapter will help you to develop a systematic approach to fault finding. The flowcharts are not intended to be the only approach, and are not always the most appropriate method to adopt, but are useful as a guide to training the way you think. They are not a substitute for not knowing the system and how it works.

Flowcharts are a common way of defining steps in a process using symbols in a graphical representation. The charts outlined for troubleshooting use three basic symbols, a circle/oval to represent the start or end of the process, a square for instructions/explanation, and a diamond for questions. To use each flowchart, start at the top and follow the arrowed lines through the chart, taking the relevant route.

*ASSUMPTIONS*

The troubleshooting flowcharts are included on the basis of a few simple assumptions made about your experience with PCs. Take time to consider these and decide whether you need to take further action.

❏ You are familiar with the use of software, basic DOS commands, the function of main system components, and the operation of the system.

❏ You can use basic tools and test equipment. This includes testmeters used to measure voltage and *resistance*. I have deliberately not included such explanations since they are covered very effectively in almost any introductory electronics book.

❏ You are fully aware of the necessary safety precautions when working on PCs.

**Table 7.6**  Troubleshooting flowcharts

| Reference | Description |
|---|---|
| TF1: Start-up | Covers the first stages following switching on the supply and leads on to other flowcharts. |
| TF2: System | An overview of system components that may appear to be related to the power supply. |
| TF3: Display | Provides the basic steps for testing associated with incorrect displays. |
| TF4: No POST | If the POST does not appear to run this flowchart will guide you through the most appropriate test procedures. |
| TF5: Boot-up | Designed to assist with troubleshooting the boot process following on from the POST. |
| TF6: Hard disk drive | Troubleshooting the hard disk drive which will not boot from the system files. |
| TF7: Floppy disk drive | Troubleshooting the floppy disk drive which cannot be accessed. |
| TF8: Serial port | Basic steps in assessing problems with the mouse or other serial port peripherals. |
| TF9: Parallel port | Basic steps in assessing problems with the printer or other parallel port peripherals. |
| TF10: Power supply | The final steps in assessing the condition of the power supply. |

*USING THE FLOWCHARTS*

Table 7.6 lists all of the troubleshooting flowcharts from the following pages and gives a brief overview of their purpose.

*TF1: START-UP*

The first action after visual checks is to switch on the system and run the POST. In this test there are basically four possible outcomes.

❏ The system is 'dead', no indication of anything working. In this case the flow-chart indicates following through with chart TF2 for the System.
❏ There are signs of life but the POST did not appear to run. TF4 can be used to investigate problems with No POST.
❏ POST appears to run but the monitor display is incorrect: indicates checking the display using chart TF3.
❏ POST runs and either displays an error code indicating the suspect device, or passes on to the Boot process.

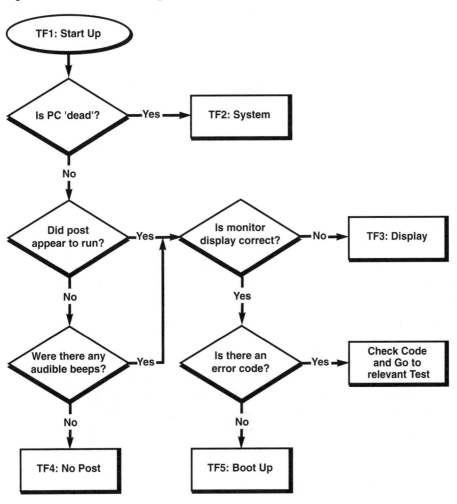

*TF2: SYSTEM*

The outcomes from this test should indicate the area within the system that is suspect.

❑ One outcome is that of a faulty power supply. For this you are directed to TF10: Power supply.

❑ If the fault results from a peripheral or adaptor card, that device should be identified by selective disconnection as described in the later stages of the chart.

---

It is important to note that not all power supplies react in the same way. Early AT system power supplies were supplied with a large load resistor which allowed the supply to operate without a hard disk drive connected. In these systems if the system board and internal devices were all disconnected the supply could be damaged. In some more modern supplies if the system board and devices are all disconnected the supply shuts down and will not operate. In either of these examples, you should use a dummy load connected to the power supply which should consist of suitable high-power resistors. This is good practice anyhow! Seek the advice of an electronics technician who should be able to help. If a dummy load cannot be arranged your alternative is to use a known good device as a load substitute.

---

* Where reference is made in any of the flowcharts to disconnecting the power supply from the rest of the system you should consider these points.


*TF3: DISPLAY*

For a system that appears to have completed the POST, and even booted, but produces an incorrect display check the monitor, including the brightness and contrast controls, and the cables. This can sometimes save time since many problems in this area are as a result of dislodged cables. There are three basic stages in this test.

1. The monitor appears to be dead, the screen and power LEDs are dark as if switched off. If there is no problem with either the mains cable or the fuse in the mains plug, it requires the attention of an expert. The insides of a monitor are potentially more dangerous then the insides of the power supply.
2. If the monitor is attempting to work but text is not visible, or is corrupted, the first suspects are the signal cable and connectors.
3. If the cable and connector are OK check the video adaptor, then the system board.

If the POST indicates a video adaptor card problem, it can be assumed that the monitor and connecting cable are OK.

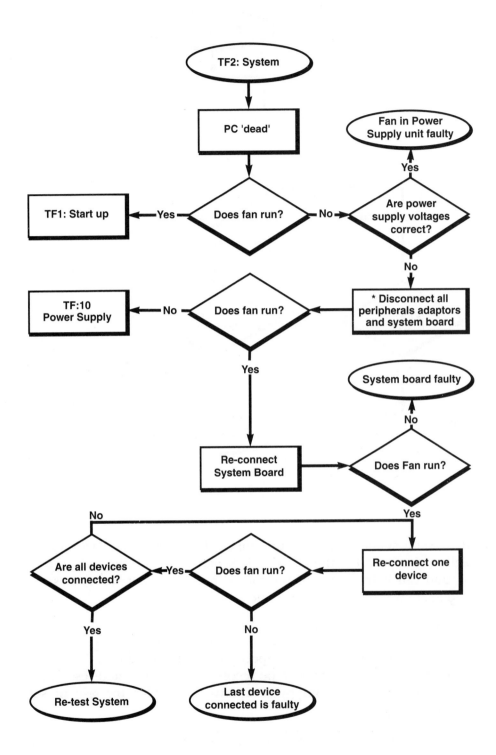

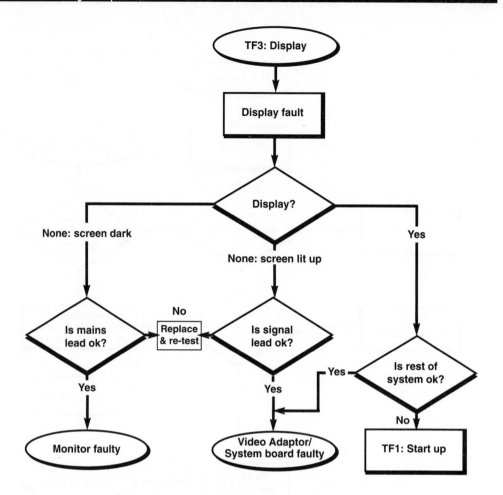

*TF4: NO POST*

Working on a system that does not appear to run the POST can lead you to virtually any area within the PC. The flowchart takes you through several basic steps, and can help in identifying the suspect area, but sometimes the only solution is to use advanced diagnostic tools.

1. Eliminate the power supply and ensure that there is some life in the system.
2. Disconnect all devices other than the system board, keyboard and monitor. If POST still fails to run then suspect the system board.
3. If POST runs, each device can be reconnected in turn and tested; if access can be gained to the floppy disk drive it enables the use of software diagnostics.

See notes in TF2 with reference to running the power supply without load.

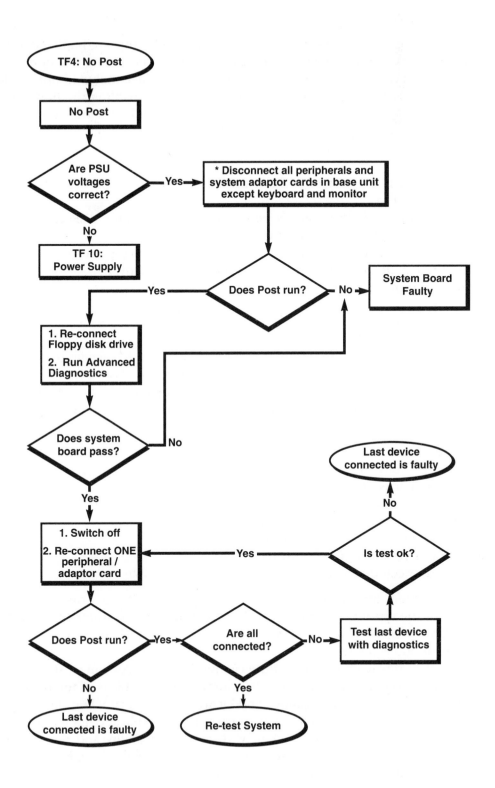

*TF5: BOOT-UP*

The boot process assumes an active monitor display and a completed POST without errors. The next step is to establish whether the system will boot from a disk drive. Remember the advanced CMOS set-up which included options for selecting the sequence of drives for system boot and enabling the floppy disk drive? This is a good point at which to check that the configuration has not been modified. There are four basic outcomes from this test, eventually resulting in a fully operational system if faults are not detected.

1. If the system will not boot from the hard disk drive you are referred to flowchart TF6.
2. If the floppy disk drive cannot be accessed, assuming the diskette is not at fault, TF7 may provide some answers.
3. Once the system has booted from a disk drive the final pieces of the jigsaw are the parallel and serial ports, TF9 and TF8, respectively.
4. An operational system?

*TF6: HARD DISK DRIVE*

The main steps involve determining whether the fault is specific to the hard disk drive, or general to all drives. A similar approach should be adopted to fault finding with CD-ROM drives. The following checks should be made when troubleshooting on either type, before continuing with more detailed inspection.

❑ Is the drive active – is it clicking or whirring?
❑ Check power connector voltages.
❑ Confirm correct configuration of CMOS set-up.
❑ Check that all connectors are plugged in correctly.
❑ Check for damaged or incorrect polarity of leads.
❑ Check that drive adaptor cards are seated correctly.
❑ Check drive-select jumpers/switches.
❑ Run advanced diagnostic test for disk drives if possible.

If the problem appears to be intermittent, especially if it gets worse with time, check that the system is well ventilated and airflow is not restricted by dirt or a faulty fan. Excessive heat building up can encourage the disk drive to perform all sorts of odd activities.

Other than replacing the drive, little can be done if a problem exists with the heads, voice coil activator or major disk surface defect. This is in the main due to the specialist tools, test facilities and clean area essential when dismantling hard drives. It is not recommended to carry out internal repairs to the drive unless you are completely confident with your own ability and the facilities available. Substitution is often the easiest method of establishing faulty drives, cables or controllers if suitable replacements are available.

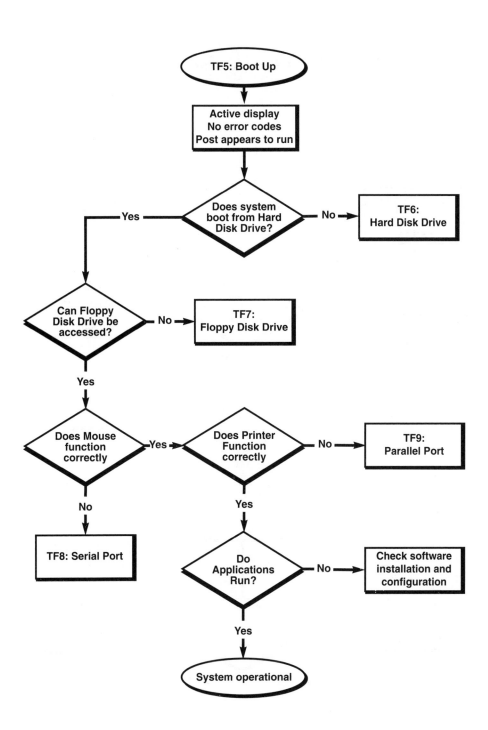

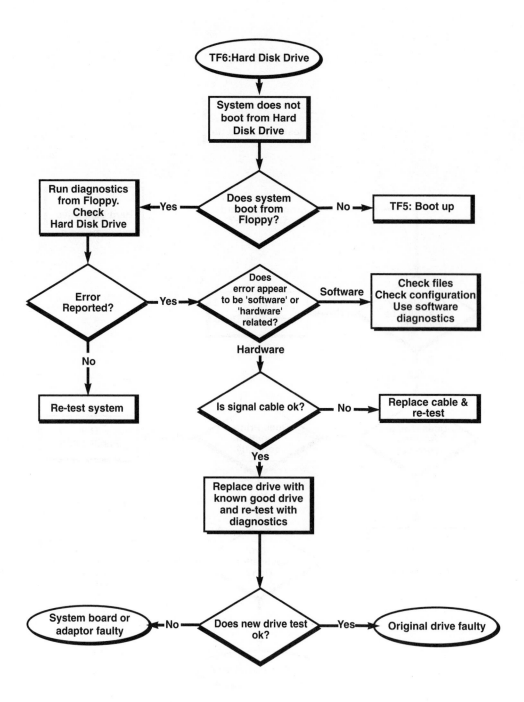

TF6:Hard Disk Drive

System does not boot from Hard Disk Drive

Does system boot from Floppy?

Yes → Run diagnostics from Floppy. Check Hard Disk Drive

No → TF5: Boot up

Error Reported?

Yes → Does error appear to be 'software' or 'hardware' related?

Software → Check files Check configuration Use software diagnostics

No → Re-test system

Hardware

Is signal cable ok?

No → Replace cable & re-test

Yes

Replace drive with known good drive and re-test with diagnostics

Does new drive test ok?

No → System board or adaptor faulty

Yes → Original drive faulty

## *TF7: FLOPPY DISK DRIVES*

See general notes included in TF6: Hard disk drives. In addition to this advice you should always double check the diskette. Is it OK, the correct format, write protected, etc.? There are problems associated with diskettes that cannot be determined with diagnostic tools, and can only be described as a result of user error. These types of error should be carefully evaluated before diving in to start stripping the system. Some of the more common errors are summarized in Table 7.7.

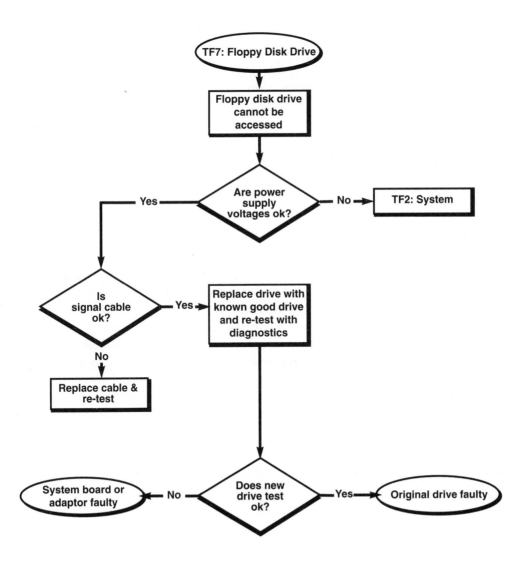

**Table 7.7**  Diskette errors

| Error | Description |
|---|---|
| Access denied | An attempt has been made to erase a write-protected file, or to read a non-existent file |
| Drive not ready | Disk not inserted or drive door is open |
| General failure error drive $x$ | Incompatible disk, e.g. unformatted |
| Insufficient disk space | Not enough free space on target disk |
| Bad command or file name | Command not recognized by DOS or file does not exist |
| Write protect error drive $x$ | Target disk is write-protected |
| Abort, Retry, Ignore, Fail? | Select 'abort' to terminate operation; select 'retry' to correct error and try again; select 'ignore' to ignore the error and continue if possible; select 'fail' to revert to valid drive |

*TF8 AND 9: SERIAL AND PARALLEL PORTS*

Faults arising with serial and parallel ports tend to be based upon faulty peripherals, incorrect configuration, poor cables or connectors, faulty adaptor cards or conflicts arising with IRQ or DMA channels. The latter are usually linked to the incorrect addition of more adaptors.

Assuming that the configuration has been checked and is correct, there are two basic questions. Is the fault a result of an external peripheral (mouse or printer), or is the fault internal to the system? This is where advanced diagnostic tools are invaluable because of their ability to test the internal workings using loop-back plugs which eliminate the need for peripheral connection. The flowcharts will help to determine which of these areas is most likely, and recommend replacements.

The golden rule is to check all connected peripherals before anything else.

❏ Is the printer switched on and full of ink and paper?
❏ Is the mouse OK?

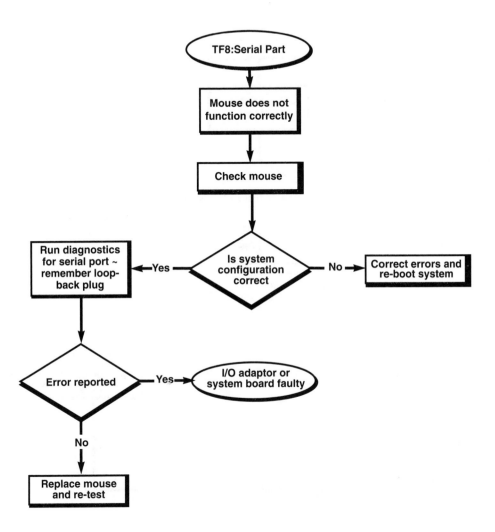

TF8:Serial Part

Mouse does not function correctly

Check mouse

Run diagnostics for serial port ~ remember loop-back plug ◄—Yes— Is system configuration correct —No►► Correct errors and re-boot system

Error reported —Yes►► I/O adaptor or system board faulty

No

Replace mouse and re-test

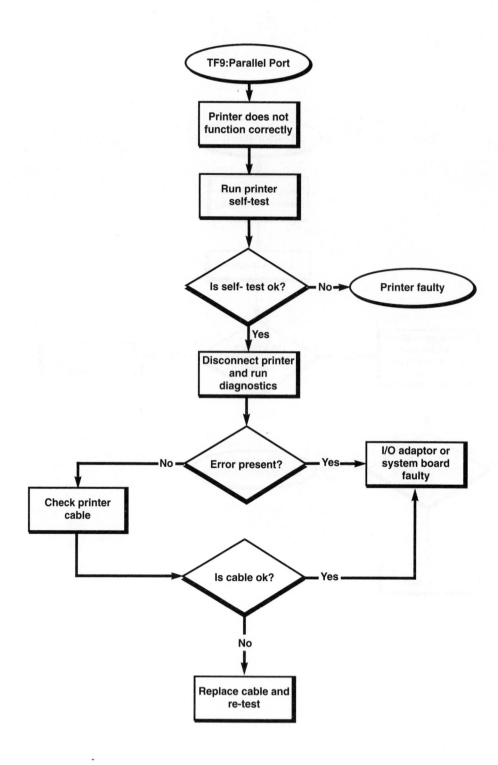

*TF10: POWER SUPPLY*

Although this is the last of the flowcharts, if the power supply is suspect you will have bypassed most of the other charts to reach this stage. There are no signs of life in the PC, all devices are disconnected from the power supply, and the voltages are incorrect. Your basic test is to establish whether the mains cable is faulty. This is achieved by testing for *continuity*, or by substitution. Although there are internal fuses in some power supplies, these should not be checked by non-qualified persons.

> **The power supply is a complex electronic circuit and the cover should not be removed by non-qualified persons.**

Refer to the notes in TF2 with reference to running the power supply without a load. With a dummy load connected, or a known good system board, if the voltages revert to the correct values, then the power supply is probably OK, and you need to refer back to earlier flowcharts.

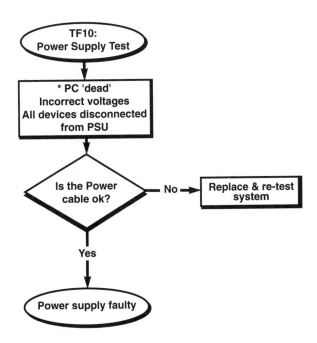

# Additional notes on fault finding

*SYSTEM BOARD*

Failure of the system board can be difficult to detect and even more difficult to repair other than by replacing socketed components, unless specialist equipment is available. Consideration should only be given to the system board when all other avenues have been examined. Fault finding on the system board should be divided into the main components of the board that are easily accessed: the microprocessor, ROM BIOS, memory chips, cache and possibly the CMOS back-up battery.

If the system board is suspect take the following initial steps.

❑ Ensure that all connectors, chips, SIMMS, etc., are plugged in correctly.
❑ Check that the board is clean and free from foreign bodies.
❑ Confirm the system configuration if possible.
❑ Remove unnecessary components, e.g. memory above 1 Mb.
❑ Run a system board test from an advanced diagnostic utility.
❑ Check any error codes displayed.
❑ Replace or repair as necessary.

Microprocessors and BIOS are both reliable and expensive in modern systems. Troubleshooting problems associated with these devices can be very taxing unless you are very familiar with system operations. Very often if problems do ever arise, it tends to be in ageing systems which, owing to software application demands, are probably in need of upgrade. When this is the case it is often more cost effective to replace the entire system board.

*MEMORY*

Defective memory will normally be encountered during the POST procedure. An error code may appear on the screen, but only briefly, followed by a parity check display. The screen should be watched closely after power-on, to make a note of any error before it is replaced by other text. Faults in the first block of memory can prevent the system from booting; if this occurs there is usually still an audible error code produced.

Preliminary checks are similar to those already discussed.

❑ Check system configuration.
❑ Check CONFIG.SYS and AUTOEXEC.BAT files for irregularities.
❑ Check that chips are inserted correctly, and of the correct specification.
❑ Check for foreign bodies.

Opinions vary, but in my experience, any chip that is mounted in one of the older type sockets is subject to 'chip creep'. If suspect, remove the chip, clean contacts and refit. This applies to DRAM, SIPs, and to a lesser extent SIMMs. It is unlikely that you should experience this problem with modern socket styles.

*CMOS BACK-UP BATTERY*

Problems encountered with the CMOS back-up battery will usually come to light through the frustrating task of correcting CMOS information every time the PC has not been used for some time. The battery loses its charge and the contents of CMOS are lost. It is important that if the battery is replaced the correct type is used, and connected the correct way round. If you have a system where the battery is housed inside a chip, it will be necessary to replace the chip itself.

*KEYBOARDS*

Problems with keyboards may relate to the actual keyboard, the connecting lead, or less often the controller. Before performing detailed tests, it is advisable to check the following.

❏ Check that the keyboard is plugged in, and of the correct type – if not, a relevant message is usually displayed.
❏ Check that keys are not stuck down, especially the cursors, shift, enter, Ctrl and Alt keys.
❏ Observe the POST carefully, and make a note of error codes.
❏ If a 3xx code is preceded by a HEX number, this is the *scan code* for the failed key switch.
❏ Run an advanced diagnostic keyboard test.
❏ In many systems if a known good keyboard is substituted, and the fault still persists, remove the keyboard plug and check the voltages at the keyboard connector on the system board. If the voltages are not within the specification listed in Table 7.8, the fault lies with either the controller or the system board.

If a fault exists on the keyboard which is more than a stuck key or dirty key switch, it is often more economical to replace the entire keyboard.

**Table 7.8** Voltages on keyboard connector

| Pin | Voltage (V) | |
| --- | --- | --- |
| | Min | Max |
| 1 | +2.0 | +5.5 |
| 2 | +4.8 | +5.5 |
| 3 | +2.0 | +5.5 |
| 4 | Ground 0 V | |
| | +2.0 | +5.5 |

*IRQ/DMA CONFLICT*

In many cases, conflict between adaptor cards involving interrupt requests and DMA channels will result in a major shutdown of the system. It is important that any new cards introduced into a system do not disturb the existing configuration by using the same IRQ or DMA channels. Observe the following precautions whenever making changes to adaptors within a system.

❏ When adding additional adaptors always check the address and IRQ/DMA settings of the manufacturer's default settings for the card with the documentation for the existing system.
❏ When troubleshooting conflicts, start with a basic system, i.e. remove all unnecessary cards, and add them one at a time until the fault occurs.
❏ If the fault appears after an upgrade, return the system to its original state and test the operation to establish whether the fault is a result of the added device.

## Summary

Troubleshooting computers is a complicated business. The best technicians are those with a great range of varying experiences from which to draw. This chapter has provided the tools and the opportunity to enable you to gain some of that experience. Continued reference to the flowcharts and relevant sections of other chapters will help you to build confidence and improve your understanding of the wonderful world of PCs.

Self-assessment questions are not included in this chapter. My philosophy is that the best learning method is to get out there and do it. Find those faulty systems and put your troubleshooting skills to the test.

## Basic jargon

*Burn-in.* The continued running of electronic equipment over a long period of time.
*Continuity.* A continuous connection. Associated closely with resistance in terms of measuring the continuity of cable and fuses. Good continuity = low resistance; poor continuity = high resistance.
*LED.* A light emitting diode is an electronic indicator used in a similar way to an indicator bulb.
*Loop-back plug.* A pre-wired plug used in I/O sockets to simulate a peripheral device.
*Resistance.* The opposition to the flow of electrical current. Measured in Ohms ($\Omega$). The lower the resistance, the more current flows. Cables and fuses should have low resistance, just a few Ohms.
*Scan code.* Keyboard scan code is a numerical code that identifies specific keys.

# 8
# Practical exercises

## Introduction

This section contains a series of exercises that will help to clarify the knowledge and understanding gained in earlier sections. It begins by looking at the range of component parts making up a standard PC, leading on to an appreciation of the various techniques involved in upgrading.

The repair of a modern PC is usually taken to component level, where the component is often described as a field replaceable unit (FRU). As implied, this is not normally an individual electronic component, but a circuit board or peripheral device. Very often the cost involved in repairing one of these FRUs is more than the cost of a replacement unit. A first step towards the maintenance of a PC is through the identification and understanding of these FRUs.

There are several basic FRUs within a typical system:

- case and power supply
- keyboard
- monitor
- mouse
- floppy disk drive
- hard disk drive
- CD-ROM
- system board including microprocessor, memory and BIOS
- expansion adaptor cards for video, parallel and serial outputs, and disk drive.

Any one of these components could cause problems. In reality the devices that tend to produce most headaches are those that use mechanical parts, such as the keyboard or disk drives.

# Types of PC used

Throughout the exercises the guidance and supporting notes are based mainly on a standard type PC. It is important for the reader to be reminded that the range of PCs available is extensive, and that no two models are necessarily identical. Some judgement is therefore essential when using the notes or instructions in the following practical and upgrading exercises. The golden rule is: if in doubt, find out!

It is assumed throughout that the installed operating system is DOS.

*SYSTEM VARIATIONS*

For the purpose of these exercises, the model of PC used in diagrams is that of a typical desktop IBM clone. The internal layout of system board, adaptor cards and drives follows a style typical of many modern PCs, but not common to all.

In order to assist users of different system layouts, at the end of each exercise there is included a section showing variations that may occur in other models such as a tower case systems and the non-clone varieties.

# Using the exercises

Throughout this chapter you will find a range of terminology used in supporting descriptions and instructions for both the exercises and upgrading guides. The background to this is provided in the following pages and should be read carefully before continuing.

*ENTERING COMMANDS*

When an instruction reads 'Enter the command: MSD', it means literally type, using the keyboard, the letter 'M', followed by the letter 'S' and then 'D'. These should then appear on the screen after the prompt.

An instruction enclosed by chevrons < > is actioned immediately by pressing the appropriate key indicated, e.g. <Ret> means press the 'Return' or 'Enter' key, and <Del> means press the 'Delete' key.

The individual letters 'Ret' or 'Del' must not be typed.

*INSTRUCTOR NOTES*

For the benefit of tutors, instructors, or other individuals offering guidance, I have included towards the end of some exercises additional notes, aimed at further explanation of the exercise. These might include the aims of the exercise or highlight some of the limitations involved.

*SOFTWARE UTILITIES*

The exercises have deliberately been limited to the use of readily available and affordable utilities. These include

• the use of CMOS set-up to obtain configuration information
• various DOS utilities found on any DOS installation
• Microsoft Diagnostics (MSD).

Other packages such as those mentioned in Chapter 6, e.g. Post-probe and Norton utilities, would be of great value, but it is assumed that these are not available, and hence they are not included in the exercises.

*STEPS*

Instructions for the exercises and guides are provided in a series of steps, an example of which is shown below. Each numbered step gives the instruction, with the remainder of the text offering advice. Both of these sections should be read carefully before carrying out the step described.

## 9. Indicates the next step in the exercise and provides instructions

📖 Provides references to other chapters, or additional technical information that will help in understanding the task involved in this step.

💻 Provides feedback information about the task in hand. This may be advice on the best way to tackle the step, or may make comment on what is expected as a result of the step.

*TABLES*

Throughout the exercises tables are provided to record relevant information for future reference. These are small and illustrate only an example of the type of table to use. Full-size versions are reproduced in Appendix B for your personal use.

Example of an instruction step

# Exercise 1 – FRU identification

This exercise is specifically designed to be used in a training situation by the instructor or tutor. If this does not apply to you then I would advise collecting as many old, surplus parts of a PC as possible from computer fairs and boot sales, and then have a go at identifying them.

**Aim:** You will be provided with 10 components that may be described as FRUs, each one labelled with a number. Your aim is to identify each FRU and provide basic functional details.

*INSTRUCTOR NOTES*

This exercise is provided as a method of helping students to identify component parts of a PC without the components being *in situ*. Being very much open ended, the instructor has the flexibility to apply the exercise to a range of different hardware and systems.

**1. Using the information provided in this book, or from your own experience, complete Table 8.1, taking care to include as much information as possible about each unit.**

Terms used to describe the function of the unit may include disk drive, adaptor card, and memory, but when asked to complete the type of unit you should be more specific.

For each of the components provided in the exercise, you might like to consider answers to the following questions as a beginning:

| | |
|---|---|
| Disk drives: | Is it a floppy or hard (fixed) drive?<br>What is its capacity?<br>What make and model?<br>Do you need additional data for set up, e.g. number of tracks, sectors? |
| Adaptor cards: | What type of card is it?<br>Is it multifunction?<br>Do any sockets help in identification?<br>What type of expansion bus does it use?<br>What 'bit size' is it? |
| System board: | The processor: type, speed?<br>Memory: type, capacity, speed? |

**Table 8.1** FRU identification

| Unit reference | Function of unit | Type of unit | Comments |
|---|---|---|---|
| 1 | | | |
| 2 | | | |
| 3 | | | |
| 4 | | | |
| 5 | | | |
| 6 | | | |
| 7 | | | |
| 8 | | | |
| 9 | | | |
| 10 | | | |

# Exercise 2 – Preparation

**Aim:** This exercise will introduce the tasks of recording basic system information. Part 1 covers basic information and Part 2 helps you to complete
the System Documentation form essential for **all** systems.

*PART 1: SYSTEM INFORMATION*

Before commencing with this exercise, ensure that all necessary components are
present and connected correctly including Test Disk 1 (see Chapter 7).

---

**1. Turn on the PC and monitor. The mains switch may be a push-
button type mounted on the front panel, or a toggle switch at
the rear of the system on the right-hand side panel. After a few
moments, power-on test information should be displayed, and
all the disk drives should be activated sequentially. Eventually
the command prompt will appear and all other activity cease.**

Command prompt: `c:\>` assumes the system has booted in DOS.

---

**2. Place the test disk in the disk drive.**

---

**3. At the command prompt enter the command: a: <Ret>**

A new command prompt will now appear, `a:\` , indicating that the system
is ready for access to drive A.

---

Before continuing it is essential to identify and record important information
about the system. This can be achieved using a variety of software, an example
of which is the Microsoft Diagnostics (MSD) command on the utilities disk.

Although the software can be used to access quite complex information about
your system, at this stage DO NOT access any information other than that indicated below.

---

**4. Enter the command: MSD <Ret>**

After taking a few seconds for MSD to load, the display should look similar
to that shown in Fig. 8.1. If not, consult your instructor.

---

**5. From the display, record the relevant information in Table 8.2.**

A reminder that a full-size table is provided in Appendix B for recording the
information.

---

**6. When complete, exit MSD by pressing the key <F3>.**

The system should now return to the command prompt for drive A.

In old-style hard disk drives, when switching off the mechanism had to be 'parked' to prevent the heads from coming into contact with the disk surface and causing damage. On modern drives this is achieved automatically and should not concern you. If in doubt consult your system or drive manual.

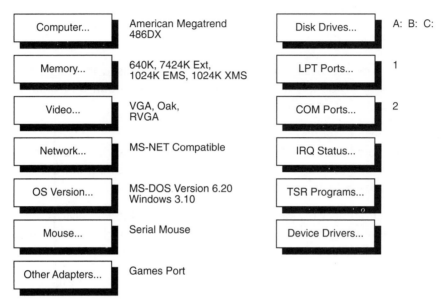

**Fig. 8.1** Typical MSD display

**Table 8.2** System summary

| System information | Comments |
| --- | --- |
| Computer | |
| Base memory | |
| Extended memory | |
| Expanded memory | |
| Video | |
| Network | |
| OS version | |
| Mouse | |
| Disk drives | |
| LPT ports (parallel) | |
| COM ports (serial) | |

*PART 2: RECORDING SYSTEM CONFIGURATION*

One of the simplest methods of obtaining such information is to use a software diagnostic package such as MSD and the System Documentation form in Appendix B7.

## 1. Load MSD as described earlier, and complete the System Documentation form using the following guidelines for each block of information on the form.

**Block 1:** PC identification.

⌨ Block 1 on the System Documentation form is used to record basic details
necessary in identifying the PC. This information can be obtained from the
manufacturer's identification plate.

**Block 2:** System details
    – microprocessor and memory information is available from the main menu
    – press <P> to select 'computer' for information about the BIOS
(press <Esc> to return to main menu).

⌨ Physical details about the type of memory fitted (SIPs, SIMMs, etc.) can only
be obtained by looking inside. Complete this part later when removing the
cover in Exercise 4.

**Block 3:** Hard disk drives – select disk drives from the main menu by pressing
the letter <D>
    (press <Esc> to return to main menu).

⌨ The main details needed at this stage are capacity, number of heads, sectors
and cylinders. Information relating to the manufacturer and interface can only
be obtained once the cover is removed, or from the drive manual.

**Block 4:** Floppy disk drives – once again the same disk drive menu is used by
selecting 'D' from the main menu
    (press <Esc> to return to main menu).

⌨ The slot position of the adaptor card used for the disk drives can only be
determined once the cover is removed.

**Block 5:** Parallel ports
    – press <L> to select 'LPT Ports' (Esc. to return)
    – press <Q> to select 'IRQ Status'
    (press <Esc> to return to main menu).

⌨ 'LPT Ports' is used to determine the base address. 'IRQ Status' is used to
determine the interrupt request associated with each parallel port. The type
of peripheral attached, if any, is established by identifying the device that is
connected to the adaptor card connector, e.g. printer.

**Block 6:** Serial ports
- press <C> to select 'COM Ports' (Esc. to return)
- press <Q> to select 'IRQ Status'
(press <Esc> to return to main menu).

 'COM Ports' is used to determine the base address. 'IRQ Status' is used to determine the interrupt request associated with each serial port. The type of peripheral attached, if any, is established by identifying the device that is connected to the adaptor card connector, e.g. mouse, modem.

**Block 7:** Adaptor information – look at the rear of the system base unit to determine the types of adaptors fitted.

The identity of some of the adaptor cards fitted can be established from the types of sockets on the rear panel of the base unit. Once recognized their position can be recorded on the form against the appropriate slot.

Some adaptors unfortunately cannot be identified, or their position located, until the cover is removed. Once adaptors are identified, the information gained earlier in the exercise can be transferred to this part of the form.

**Block 8:** CONFIG.SYS
- select 'FILE' from the title bar
- select CONFIG.SYS from the menu
- write down all of the information on to the form.
(press <Esc> to return to main menu).

Selecting 'File' from the main menu is achieved using the mouse, or by pressing <Alt+F> together. CONFIG.SYS can then be viewed by selecting with the mouse, the cursor keys, or by pressing the number <2>. Care must be taken in writing down the information, as it is important that this is accurately recorded.

**Block 9:** AUTOEXEC.BAT
- select 'File' from the title bar
- select AUTOEXEC.BAT from the menu
- write down all of the information on to the form
When complete, exit MSD by pressing the key <F3>.

From the 'File' menu, accessed in the same way as in Block 8, select AUTOEXEC.BAT using the mouse or cursor keys, or by pressing a different number, <1>.

All of the basic information needed to maintain your system in the future should now be recorded, other than that requiring the removal of the cover. Continue with the exercises, and when access is gained to the inside of the base unit, return to your System Documentation form and complete the final details.

# Exercise 3 – Preparation for disassembly

**Aim:** This exercise will produce a record of all external connections to the system. The record can be used later in reassembly.

*INSTRUCTOR NOTES*

Although a simple exercise in itself, the main purpose is to build on experiences gained in Exercise 1 and enable the user to appreciate the range and importance of connectors used in the assembly of a PC. It should be noted that because of the way in which the system operates, MSD does not always record the IRQ assignments accurately. This becomes important when using systems with many peripherals attached.

1. **Switch off the mains supply both on the PC and at the mains supply outlet.**

2. **From the rear of the system base unit, disconnect the mains plug from its socket, and the monitor mains supply plug if used.**

3. **Move the PC so that the rear panel can be observed.**

4. **Record in Table 8.3 details of every cable connected to the PC.**

Record the function of the connection, where each is connected, and the type of connector used, e.g. nine-pin plug, 15-pin socket. Note that in order to record this information, you will need to remove each connector. Do so one connector at a time, using the correct tools as necessary. Use Fig. 8.2 and the variation notes for guidance.

**Table 8.3** Rear panel connections

| Expansion slot position | Function or application | Connector type |
| --- | --- | --- |
| 0 | | |
| 1 | | |
| 2 | | |
| 3 | | |
| 4 | | |
| 5 | | |
| 6 | | |
| 7 | | |

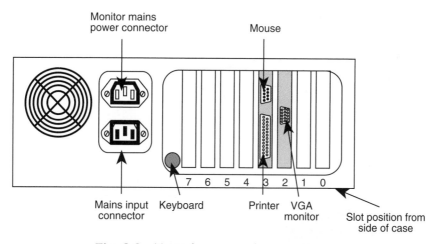

**Fig. 8.2** Typical rear panel connections

*SYSTEM VARIATIONS*

See Fig. 8.3.

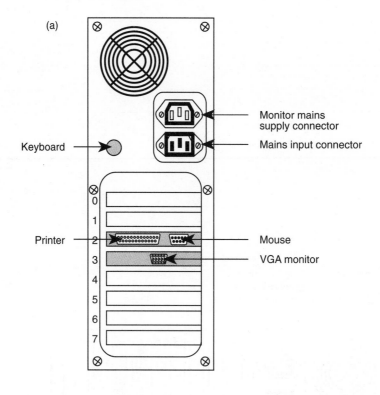

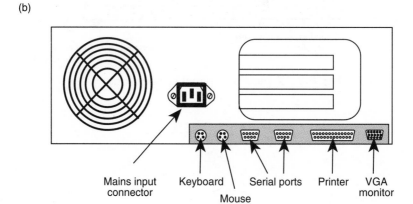

**Fig. 8.3** Rear panel connections for (a) tower case system; (b) compatible system

# Exercise 4 – Removing the cover

**Aim:** A very short exercise providing simple guidance on how to remove the cover from the system base unit. The exercise concludes with a second part which looks at the internal layout and asks you to identify the main FRUs within the unit.

## 1. Remove the retaining screws indicated in Fig. 8.4, and store safely.

Again use the system variation notes if your system is not the same as outlined in Fig. 8.4. Store the screws safely!

## 2. Gently slide the cover backwards and upwards, taking care not to catch any internal cables. Store the cover safely to one side.

## 3. Using Fig. 8.5 as a reference, locate and identify the following components where applicable.

Use the tick boxes in Table 8.4 as a record of your findings.

Use Chapter 2 – Inside the Box to help.

**Table 8.4** Record of internal components

| | |
|---|---|
| ☐ Power supply | ☐ Expansion slots |
| ☐ System board | ☐ Video/graphics adaptor |
| ☐ Floppy disk drive(s) | ☐ Disk drive adaptor and cables |
| ☐ Hard disk drive(s) | ☐ Serial and parallel port adaptors |
| ☐ CD-ROM | ☐ Loudspeaker |

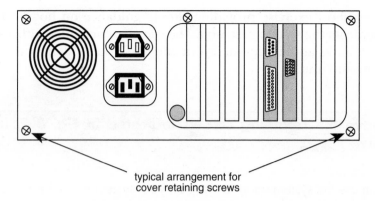

typical arrangement for
cover retaining screws

**Fig. 8.4**   Rear panel view: cover retaining screws

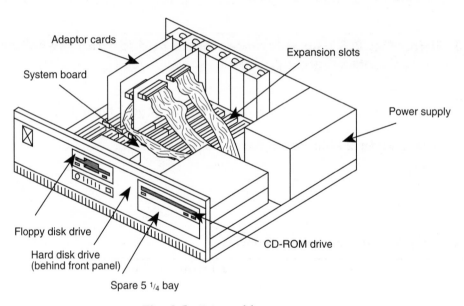

Adaptor cards

Expansion slots

System board

Power supply

Floppy disk drive

CD-ROM drive

Hard disk drive
(behind front panel)

Spare 5 ¼ bay

**Fig. 8.5**   Internal layout

*SYSTEM VARIATIONS*

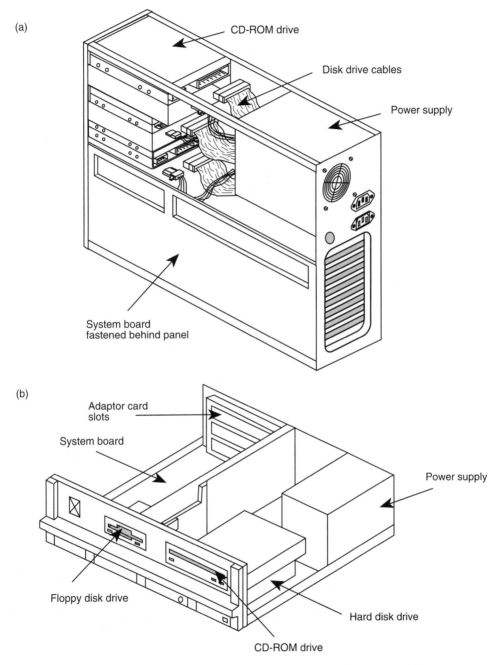

(a)

CD-ROM drive

Disk drive cables

Power supply

System board
fastened behind panel

(b)

Adaptor card
slots

System board

Power supply

Floppy disk drive

Hard disk drive

CD-ROM drive

**Fig. 8.6** Internal layout of (a) tower case system; (b) compatible system

# Exercise 5 – System disassembly

**Aim:** To become familiar with, and learn how to disassemble the main component parts of the system base unit.

Disassembling the complete system base unit is an unlikely occurrence, unless upgrading to a modern case, or making other major improvements. It is still a very effective way of getting to know the main component parts of the system and how they physically connect together.

---
**Safety Warning**
**Please observe STATIC PRECAUTIONS whilst handling computer boards, components and devices. When disconnecting leads, handle by the PLUG and NOT the CABLE.**

---

*SWITCH OFF*

## 1. Ensure that the power is turned off, and all external leads are disconnected.

*REMOVAL OF ADAPTOR CARDS*

## 2. Carefully remove all adaptors

– remove any connecting cables from the cards
– remove retaining screws
– withdraw adaptors vertically.

Figure 8.7 illustrates the position of the retaining screw, and direction of removal.

---

*REMOVAL OF DISK DRIVES*

This procedure will vary from system to system, but the basic steps are indicated in steps 3–5, and Fig. 8.8(a)–(c).

## 3. Disconnect disk drive cables (if not already done).

Before removal make sure you can identify which way round the connectors are fitted.

Care should be taken not to pull on the ribbon cable, but to pull the connector away from the drive.

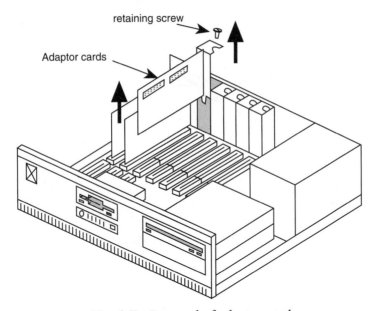

**Fig. 8.7** Removal of adaptor card

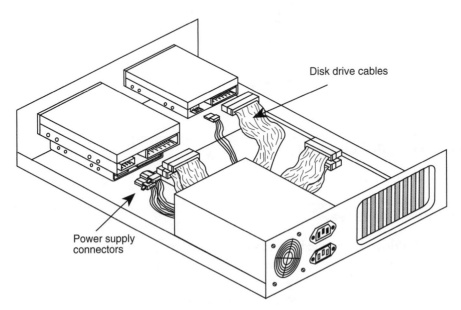

**Fig. 8.8** (a) Removal of disk drive cables

(b)

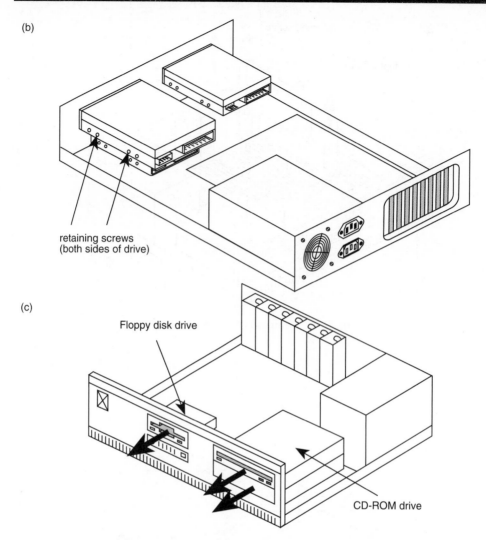

retaining screws
(both sides of drive)

(c)

Floppy disk drive

CD-ROM drive

**Fig. 8.8**   (b) Removal of retaining screws and (c) disk drive from the case

## 4. Remove retaining screws.

📖 Typical positioning of retaining screws is illustrated in Fig. 8.8(b).

## 5. Remove the drive.

💻 Slide the drive forwards from the front panel as shown by the arrows in Fig.
8.8(c). Some drives are removed 'backwards' from the panel. If the drive
cannot be removed **easily**, establish the reason why, or consult the tutor.
Place the drive in a safe, static-free location.

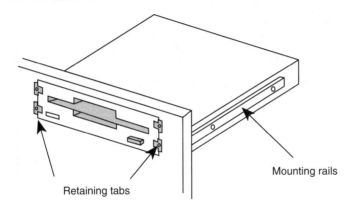

**Fig. 8.9**   Disk drive retaining tabs

*SYSTEM VARIATIONS*

Methods of mounting drives into base units can vary from system to system. Figure 8.9 illustrates a method of retaining the drive used on some older $5\frac{1}{4}$ inch drive bays which used a tab secured at either side of the front of the drive. The tabs are removed and then the drive is drawn forwards on its slide rails.

*REMOVAL OF SYSTEM BOARD*

**6. Make a note of any remaining leads and connections to the system board, i.e. loudspeaker, LED indicators.**

**7. Disconnect the leads, pulling on the connector, NOT the lead.**

These connections are shown in Fig. 8.10(a). You should be confident that you can identify each lead and its position on the board. This includes the polarity of connection.

**8. Remove any retaining screws, and slide the system board away from the power supply position, until the stand-offs disengage from the mounting slots.**

**9. Lift the board to remove.**

Typical positions for retaining screws are shown in Fig. 8.10(b). Boards vary, and some use only a single retaining screw positioned at the centre rear of the board. Under no circumstances should the board be bent or twisted, or undue pressure applied.

REMOVAL OF POWER SUPPLY

**10. Disconnect any remaining power leads.**

**11. Remove the retaining screws on the back panel.**

**12. Slide the power supply slightly forward and lift upwards out of the case.**

Typical positions for the power supply retaining screws are shown in Fig. 8.11.

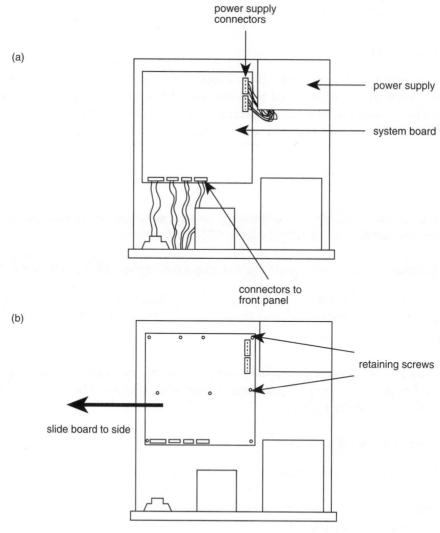

**Fig. 8.10**  (a) Connections to system board; (b) retaining screws for system board

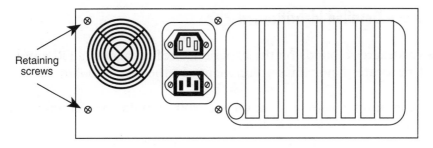

**Fig. 8.11** Retaining screws for power supply

## Exercise 6 – Detailed identification

**Aims:** This exercise builds on the experiences of recognizing FRUs in Exercise 1 by locating individual components on the system board.

Before continuing with this exercise, you should be familiar with the identification and operation of the main components within the system. Read the relevant sections of the book if you have not done so already.

### 1. Using Table 8.5 as a guide, identify and locate the listed components on the system board.

Record relevant information in the table as it is identified. Where indicated, make a note of the circuit reference number, e.g. IC4, and the type number, e.g. 80486.

**Table 8.5**  System board component identification

| Component | Present | Circuit ref. number | Type |
|---|---|---|---|
| Power connectors | | | |
| Expansion slots | | Not applicable | |
| Keyboard socket | | Not applicable | |
| Speaker connector | | Not applicable | |
| CPU chip | | | |
| Coprocessor | | | |
| ROM BIOS chip | | | |
| RAM | | | |
| Clock generator | | | |
| Crystal | | | |
| Integrated support chips | | | |
| Keyboard controller | | | |
| *Other connectors* | | | |

# Exercise 7 – System reassembly

**Aim:** To test your understanding of how the system base unit is assembled.

*PART 1: REASSEMBLY INSIDE THE CASE*

It would be very easy to say 'reassembly is simply disassembly in reverse', and 'follow Exercise 5 in reverse order'. In reality, this is essentially what you do. The basic steps are outlined below

1. **Refit the power supply and retaining screws.**

2. **Refit the system board and retaining screws.**

3. **Refit disk drives and retaining screws.**

4. **Refit adaptors and retaining screws.**

5. **Refit connecting cables.**

6. **Refit the cover.**

7. **Reconnect all external peripherals.**

1. Take care not to trap cables against the case.
2. Carefully slide the board into position and check that the stand-offs are engaged correctly. If not the bottom of the board could short against the chassis.
3. It is sometimes more convenient to reconnect cables if the drive is not secured by screws. If this practice is adopted you should take care not to displace the unrestrained drives and not forget to fit the retaining screws when finished.
4. Do not apply undue force.
5. Check that cables are seated properly and are fitted the correct way round.

*PART 2: REASSEMBLY OUTSIDE THE CASE*

The system is to be reassembled outside the case to enable further investigative work. Under these circumstances it is essential that care be taken at all times so that components are not damaged.

There is no danger of electrical shock from the power supply unit, providing the cover of the supply is **not removed**, and objects are not pushed through the air vents.

### 1. Clear an area on the work bench, and position the system board on the base provided.

The system board should be supported on an insulated board to lift it slightly from the work bench. This will help when installing the adaptor cards later. Under no circumstances should any circuit board be placed on a metal or conducting surface.

### 2. Reconnect the power supply leads.

### 3. Reconnect the keyboard.

### 4. Replace adaptors in suitable slots.

The position of adaptors might be the same as when assembled, or it might be more convenient to rearrange their positions to provide easier access to peripherals.

### 5. Reconnect ribbon cables to all disk drives.

**Note**: it is important that the disk drives remain level, do not come into contact with metal objects, and are not placed on metal surfaces.

### 6. Reconnect the monitor.

### 7. Reconnect the mains leads BUT DO NOT TURN POWER ON.

Check with your instructor before continuing. If you are not working in a training situation make absolutely sure that all connections are correct.

### 8. Turn on the power and check that the system is operating correctly, using a diagnostics package.

The system should now be reassembled safely on the work bench, and in working order.

# Exercise 8 – Changing adaptor cards

**Aim:** This exercise provides the opportunity to reflect on some of the constraints and difficulties that may arise when introducing new adaptors.

Although the removal of adaptors has already been covered in earlier exercises, it is important that the effect of adding additional cards is appreciated before moving on to upgrading systems. Reasons for changing adaptors or installing new ones can be as varied as the cards themselves. It might be a new card to upgrade the video, or a replacement multi-I/O card combining disk drive adaptor with I/O ports. Before even considering making changes to adaptors in your own system it is essential to check the compatibility of such cards and systems. It is surprising how often an adaptor will work in one system yet not in another. The solution is to buy from a reputable source, and seek confirmation of compatibility with your system before you part with hard-earned cash.

## 1. Check documentation for the existing system.

## 2. Check documentation for the new adaptor.

🖳 Comparison of the two should highlight any possible conflicts with interrupt requests or addresses. This is not such a problem if the adaptor card provides alternatives to the default value.

## 3. If appropriate, select suitable positions for jumpers or DIP switches according to manufacturer's instructions.

## 4. Remove the cover from the system base unit.

📖 Chapter 6 – System Configuration

🖳 Exercise 5 – System Disassembly

## 5. If the adaptor is additional

- find a suitable free expansion slot
- remove the blanking plate from the rear panel.

## 6. If the adaptor is a replacement

- disconnect any cables
- remove the old adaptor card.

🖳 Exercise 5 – System Disassembly.

## 7. Install the adaptor card in the slot, and reconnect any necessary cables.

🖥  Exercise 7 – Reassembly.

## 8. Test to ensure correct operation.

## 9. Replace system base unit cover

📖  Chapter 7 – Fault-finding Techniques.

🖥  Exercise 7 – Reassembly.

*INSTRUCTOR NOTES*

The exercise is not intended to follow directly on from the previous exercise, and assumes that the system base unit is complete and intact.

# Upgrading guide 1 – Adding a floppy disk drive

Adding a second floppy disk drive to your system is one of the easier tasks that you might undertake, and at today's prices, probably one of the cheapest.

I have made the assumption that the drive is of the standard 1.44 Mb, $3^1/_2$ inch type and is to be added to a system with a similar drive already installed. Exceptions that may occur result from the existence of 720 Kb $3^1/_2$ inch and 360 Kb/1.2 Mb $5^1/_4$ inch disk drives. The arrangements associated with these different types are well documented in a range of books and manuals, so the aim of this exercise will be to demonstrate the overall procedure for a standard system.

## 1. Check documentation for existing system.

## 2. Check documentation for new floppy disk drive.

## 3. Remove the cover from the system base unit.

Comparison of the two should confirm suitability.
Exercise 5 – System Disassembly.

## 4. Inspect the adaptor to drive cable.

The cable must have a spare connector for the new drive, and the last connector on the cable must be connected to the existing drive. This identifies the existing drive as drive A.
Chapter 2 – Inside the Box.

## 5. If appropriate, select suitable positions on the new drive for jumpers or DIP switches according to manufacturer's instructions.

Chapter 6 – System Configuration.
In most cases the default values will be suitable but check the following.
**Adaptor cables with a 'twist'**
(a) if the jumpers are labelled DS0 DS1 DS2 DS3, select DS0;
(b) if the jumpers are labelled DS1 DS2 DS3 DS4, select DS1.
**Adaptor cables without a 'twist'**
(a) if the jumpers are labelled DS0 DS1 DS2 DS3, select DS1;
(b) if the jumpers are labelled DS1 DS2 DS3 DS4, select DS2.
This assumes that your existing drive is selected as (a) DS0 or (b) DS1, i.e. the first drive.

### 6. Install the drive into a spare bay.

Depending on the type and size of bay available, the drive will either fit directly, or require a mounting panel as shown in Fig. 8.12. This panel is used to fit a $3\frac{1}{2}$ inch disk drive or hard disk drive into a $5\frac{1}{4}$ inch bay.

Exercise 7 – Reassembly.

### 7. Attach the disk drive ribbon cable to the drive's cable connector.

### 8. Attach the power cable.

Check the polarity – pin 1 is usually indicated by the colour-striped edge of the cable.
The power cable may need a Y-splitter if there are not sufficient connectors. On older systems you should ensure that the power supply is of sufficient power rating, at least 200 W.

### 9. Switch on the system.

### 10. Run the CMOS set-up program to configure the system to recognize the new drive.

Chapter 6 – System Configuration.
The system is likely to hesitate before producing a CMOS mismatch error. This is normal until the system has been reconfigured.
From the standard set-up menu select the type for the new drive.

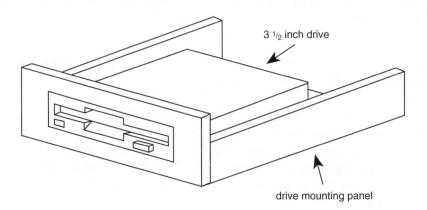

3 ½ inch drive

drive mounting panel

**Fig. 8.12**   Mounting panel for floppy disk drive

## 11. Test to ensure correct operation.

## 12. Replace base unit cover.

📖   Chapter 7 – Fault-finding Techniques.

💻   Exercise 7 – Reassembly.

## Upgrading guide 2 – Adding a hard disk drive

The basic steps in installing a second hard disk drive are very similar to those for a floppy in physical arrangements, but require a little more detail when it comes to configuration and set-up. Steps 1–9 are in effect the same as for the floppy disk drive, and steps 10–14 take you through the additional tasks. It is very important to read carefully the associated notes with each step.

### 1. Check documentation for existing system.

### 2. Check documentation for new hard disk drive.

### 3. Remove the cover from the system base unit.

⌨ Comparison of the two should confirm suitability.
Exercise 5 – System Disassembly.

### 4. Inspect the adaptor to drive cable.

⌨ The cable must have a spare connector for the new drive, and the last connector on the cable must be connected to the existing drive.
📖 Chapter 2 – Inside the Box.

### 5. Select suitable positions on the drive for jumpers according to manufacturer's instructions.

📖 ATA-IDE drives are usually configured using an options jumper block by attaching jumpers to appropriate pins on the block. The drive can be configured:
– for one or two drive operation
– to be *master* (C:) or *slave* (D:)
– to use a remote 'drive-active' LED.
The 'DS' method of drive identification as used on floppy disk drives is not used.

### 6. Install the drive into a spare bay.

⌨ Depending on the type and size of bay available, the drive will either fit directly, or require a mounting panel as shown in Fig. 8.12. This panel is used to fit a $3\frac{1}{2}$ inch disk drive or hard disk drive into a $5\frac{1}{4}$ inch bay.
Exercise 7 – Reassembly.
You may wish to leave securing the fixing screws until the drive has been connected and tested. This is useful and makes connecting cables easier, but ensure that the drive cannot be accidentally moved while testing.

## 7. Attach the disk drive ribbon cable to the drive's cable connector.

## 8. Attach the power cable.

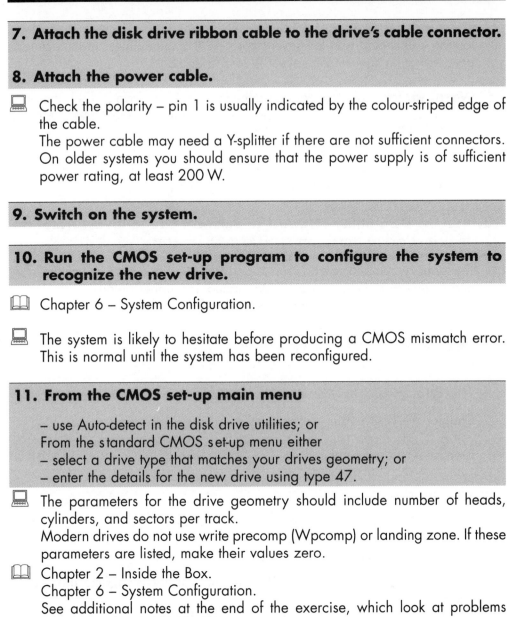 Check the polarity – pin 1 is usually indicated by the colour-striped edge of the cable.
The power cable may need a Y-splitter if there are not sufficient connectors. On older systems you should ensure that the power supply is of sufficient power rating, at least 200 W.

## 9. Switch on the system.

## 10. Run the CMOS set-up program to configure the system to recognize the new drive.

📖 Chapter 6 – System Configuration.

💻 The system is likely to hesitate before producing a CMOS mismatch error. This is normal until the system has been reconfigured.

## 11. From the CMOS set-up main menu

– use Auto-detect in the disk drive utilities; or
From the standard CMOS set-up menu either
– select a drive type that matches your drives geometry; or
– enter the details for the new drive using type 47.

💻 The parameters for the drive geometry should include number of heads, cylinders, and sectors per track.
Modern drives do not use write precomp (Wpcomp) or landing zone. If these parameters are listed, make their values zero.

📖 Chapter 2 – Inside the Box.
Chapter 6 – System Configuration.
See additional notes at the end of the exercise, which look at problems encountered with older BIOSs.

## 12. Assuming that the new drive is ATA-IDE, the next step is to partition the drive into one or more logical drives:

– run FDISK from DOS: **FDISK <ret>**
– select the option to change to drive 2
– select the option for creating a DOS partition
– select the option for creating a *primary partition*
– follow the on-screen instructions.

📖 **Warning.** Installation of MFM and RLL drives would include a *low-level* format. You should **not** low-level format an IDE drive unless manufacturer's documentation specifically says it is safe to do so.

💻 **Warning.** Take care that you select the correct drive, drive D: (2) is the slave or second drive. If you accidentally partition drive C: **YOU WILL ERASE ALL OF YOUR FILES AND DATA!**
On most systems the new drive would include a single partition using the maximum space available on the drive – primary partition. If you choose this option, FDISK completes the task and re-boot.

## 13. Run the DOS utility FORMAT to perform a high-level format on the new drive partition(s): FORMAT D: <ret>

📖 The format command can be used to perform other tasks such as volume label and system disk. Refer to your DOS manual for further details.
💻 This assumes that the operating system is DOS.

## 14. Test to ensure correct operation.

## 15. Replace base unit cover.

📖 Chapter 7 – Fault-finding Techniques.

💻 Exercise 7 – Reassembly.

---

*LIMITS TO THE BIOS*

Many older BIOSs impose limits on the values that can be used to configure hard disk drives. This in effect limits the usable size of a hard disk drive to 528 Mb. The following points can be used to help to identify the limits of your BIOS.

❏ The original BIOS in '286 and '386 systems cannot recognize more than 528 Mb.
❏ If the BIOS is dated before 1994 it will probably not recognize more than 528 Mb.

The solutions:

❏ upgrade the BIOS to a version that supports modern drives; or
❏ use a special host adaptor card that supports more than 528 Mb; or
❏ obtain software that is designed specifically to allow you to access the full capacity of your drive.

# Upgrading guide 3 – Adding a CD-ROM drive

If you can achieve success with the installation of a second hard disk drive, then the addition of a CD-ROM drive should not present any difficulties. The configuration of a CD-ROM drive is simpler, as it does not require the preparation involved with a hard disk drive.

The exercise assumes that the drive interface is standard. ATA-IDE and EIDE are now very popular and make life much simpler. If your system only has one hard disk drive, the CD-ROM can usually be used in place of a second, and is identified as drive D:. If your system already has an additional hard disk drive then an additional adaptor card will need to be installed, or the system upgraded.

### 1. Check documentation for existing system.

### 2. Check documentation for new drive (and adaptor if needed).

### 3. Remove the cover from the system base unit.

🖥 If an adaptor is to be included, comparisons should highlight any possible conflicts with interrupt requests, DMAs or addresses. This is not such a problem if the adaptor card provides alternatives to the default value. Exercise 5 – System Disassembly.

### 4. Inspect the adaptor to drive cable.

🖥 The cable must have a spare connector for the new drive, and the last connector on the cable must be connected to the existing drive. If adding a new adaptor, follow the manufacturer's instructions on installation and setting up.

📖 Chapter 2 – Inside the Box.

### 5. Select suitable positions on the drive for jumpers according to manufacturer's instructions.

### 6. If installing an adaptor select the most appropriate jumper settings for IRQ and address.

📖 Referring to the manufacturer's manual should show that this process is similar to that for a hard disk drive – ATA-IDE drives are usually configured using an options jumper block by attaching jumpers to appropriate pins on the block.

### 7. Install the drive into a spare bay.

Most CD-ROM drives are designed to fit directly into a standard $5^1/_4$ drive bay. Although the size may be different, the mounting methods are the same. Exercise 7 – Reassembly.

You may wish to leave securing the fixing screws until the drive has been connected and tested. This is useful and makes connecting cables easier, but ensure that the drive cannot be accidentally moved while testing.

### 8. Attach the drive ribbon cable to the drive's cable connector.

### 9. If using a new adaptor connect the other end of the ribbon cable the new adaptor.

### 10. Attach the power cable to the drive.

Check the polarity – pin 1 is usually indicated by the colour-striped edge of the cable.

The power cable may need a Y-splitter if there are not sufficient connectors. On older systems you should ensure that the power supply is of sufficient power rating, at least 200 W.

### 11. Switch on the system.

The system is likely to hesitate before producing a CMOS mismatch error. This is normal until the system has been reconfigured.

### 12. Follow the instructions supplied with the CD-ROM drive to run the software installation utilities.

These utilities configure the drive and the system ready for use, and are usually supplied on a $3^1/_2$ inch diskette.

### 13. Test to ensure correct operation.

### 14. Replace base unit cover.

Chapter 7 – Fault-finding Techniques.

Exercise 7 – Reassembly.

# Upgrading guide 4 – Adding a sound card

With current trends towards multimedia software, a CD-ROM usually prompts the addition of a sound card to enhance the PC's audio performance. These cards have different capabilities based upon what you want – mono, stereo, use with MIDI equipment, your stereo system, or your CD-ROM drive, and what you want to pay. Not all cards will operate with all CD-ROM drives, so consider your needs carefully. Once obtained, a sound card should be no more difficult to install than any other adaptor, but for some reason systems do sometimes develop problems. These problems can usually be attributed to the lack of attention to detail when the card is installed.

### 1. Check documentation for existing system.

### 2. Check documentation for new sound card.

Comparison of the two should highlight any possible conflicts with interrupt requests or addresses. This is not such a problem if the adaptor card provides alternatives to the default value.

The introduction of the sound card to domestic PCs is relatively new, and therefore installation can sometimes present problems with conflict and existing older cards. This makes it even more important to be sure of your existing system's configuration and set-up.

Having made that statement most sound cards today are designed to use IRQs, addresses and DMA channels not covered by the range of common devices, and should not present any difficulties.

### 3. If appropriate, select suitable positions for jumpers according to manufacturer's instructions.

### 4. Remove the cover from the system base unit.

Chapter 6 – System Configuration.
Exercise 5 – System Disassembly.

### 5. Find a suitable free expansion slot and remove the blanking plate from the rear panel.

Exercise 8 – Installing Adaptor Cards.

## 6. Install the sound card in the slot.

## 7. Connect any necessary cables and loudspeakers.

📖 Exercise 7 – Reassembly.
Exercise 8 – Installing Adaptor Cards.

## 8. Switch on the system.

💻 The system is likely to hesitate before producing a CMOS mismatch error. This is normal until the system has been reconfigured.

## 9. Follow the instructions supplied with the sound card to run the software installation utilities.

💻 These utilities configure the card and the system ready for use.
The system may need re-booting for the installation to take effect.

## 10. Test to ensure correct operation.

## 11. Replace system base unit cover.

📖 Chapter 7 – Fault-finding Techniques.

💻 Exercise 7 – Reassembly.

# Upgrading Guide 5 – Adding memory

With entry-level systems currently using 8 Mb of main memory, and software developments continuing to push requirements higher and higher, 16 Mb is becoming a very realistic option. This, together with a significant drop in prices (almost 4 Mb for the price of 1 Mb), means that it is highly probable that at some time the average PC user will want to upgrade the memory.

Main memory composed of individual DIL DRAM chips is a thing of the past, and upgrade of such systems to memory capacities of 8 and 16 Mb is totally unrealistic. The modern system uses SIMMs, and this makes upgrade comparatively easy.

## 1. Check system documentation for existing memory against your requirements.

📖 How much memory does your system have, and how much is needed by the software that you use?

## 2. Remove the cover from the system base unit.

💻 Exercise 5 – System Disassembly.

## 3. Check the system board for type and availability of sockets.

## 4. Complete Table 8.6 as a record of your findings.

📖 Chapter 5 – Memory.

💻 The following decisions have to be made:
 – are SIMMs needed in banks of 2 or 4? (Chapter 7 and Fig. 5.7)
 – can additional SIMMs be added? (Chapter 7 and Fig. 5.8)
 – do the existing SIMMs need replacing because there are no spare sockets?
 – what speed of memory is required to be compatible with the processor?
Once these questions are answered, the task of installation is fairly straightforward.

The following steps assume the use of verticaly mounted SIMMs. Figure 8.13 illustrates variations.

## 5. If replacing existing SIMMs

 – check the 'direction' of each SIMM and record
 – remove each SIMM in turn.

**Table 8.6** Evaluation of memory requirements

| Check made | Record |
|---|---|
| Microprocessor type | |
| Microprocessor speed | |
| Bus width | |
| Number of SIMM sockets | |
| Number of SIMMs installed | |
| Type of SIMMs | |
| Total memory capacity | |
| Memory requirements | |
| Additional memory needed | |
| Speed of memory needed | |

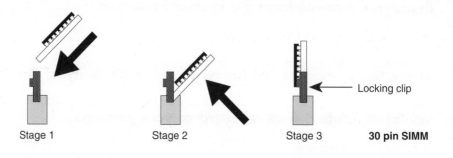

Stage 1          Stage 2          Stage 3          **30 pin SIMM**

Locking clip

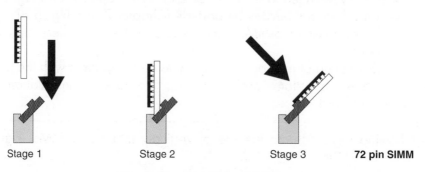

Stage 1          Stage 2          Stage 3          **72 pin SIMM**

**Fig. 8.13**   Installing SIMMs

## 6. If installing additional SIMMs, go to the next step.

⌨ The removal of a SIMM is not difficult but requires care.
Press gently outwards the retaining clips at either end of the socket. The clips and SIMM are illustrated in Fig. 8.13.
While holding the clips out, ease the module over to an angle of about 45°, and lift gently away from the socket.
Store safely in an antistatic container.

## 7. Insert a SIMM into an available socket.

## 8. Repeat the process until all modules are installed.

⌨ Figure 8.13 – comparison of 30-pin and 72-pin SIMMs..
Insert the module into the narrow channel of connections at the bottom of the socket, at an angle of about 45°.
Gently ease the module into a vertical position where it should snap into the retaining clips.
Great care must be taken that undue pressure is not applied. If the module feels restricted, **do not force**. The tiny connections in the bottom of the socket are easily damaged and very difficult to repair.
Because the SIMMs are inserted on an angle, it is usually easier to start from one end of the bank in preference to the other. The decision on which end to start from will come with a little thought and a lot of experience.

## 9. Switch on the system and allow to re-boot.

⌨ The system should identify and test the new memory for you. An incorrect memory installation will be detected by the POST.

## 10. Switch off and replace system base unit cover.

⌨ Exercise 7 – Reassembly.

## Basic jargon

*Master*. The first of two installed hard disk drives.
*Partition*. A section on a hard disk drive configured as if it were a separate drive.
*Primary partition*. The main partition on a hard disk drive.
*Slave*. The second of two installed hard disk drives.

# Appendix A
## Working safely

## Safety first

A safe working environment is essential, not only for you, but also for your computer. For your own protection you should be aware of the following points.

❑ Health and safety regulations exist for you and your workplace. Be aware of them and understand how they affect you.
❑ Never remove the cover from or attempt to repair a power supply unless you are a qualified electrical/electronics technician.
❑ Never remove the cover from or attempt to repair a monitor unless you are a qualified electrical/electronics technician.
❑ If your PC has a front panel mounted power switch then this will be the source of mains voltage. Do not remove any protective sleeving from the switch.
❑ Remove rings and watches before working on any electrical equipment.
❑ Always switch off and disconnect from the mains before working.

## Static protection

If you are one of those people who continually receives an electrical shock from the car door, then spare a thought for the poor tiny pieces of silicon inside your computer chips. Static discharge is a potential source of danger for your PC components. Static is produced by friction with some types of material such as Nylon, which causes a build-up of energy that can discharge to a metal object, e.g. your car door handle. There are three basic steps to consider when handling static-sensitive devices.

❑ Static-sensitive devices include memory, system board, chips, drives, and adaptor cards – any device with electronic components. These devices are safe when connected to the system, but are in danger when removed.

❏ Use an antistatic wrist strap. This is a special piece of wire which connects your wrist and you to a suitable earth point. The strap has an internal resistor for safety reasons.

❏ Always place removed components and devices in antistatic bags or containers. Never put them on an unprotected surface.

# *Appendix B*
# System record forms

**B1**   FRU identification (Table 8.1)

**B2**   System summary (Table 8.2)

**B3**   Rear panel connections (Table 8.3)

**B4**   Record of internal components (Table 8.4)

**B5**   System board component identification (Table 8.5)

**B6**   Evaluation of memory requirements (Table 8.6)

**B7**   System documentation (Exercise 2)

**B8**   Standard CMOS set-up display (Fig. 6.1)

**Appendix B1** FRU identification

| Unit reference | Function of unit | Type of unit | Comments |
|---|---|---|---|
| 1 | | | |
| 2 | | | |
| 3 | | | |
| 4 | | | |
| 5 | | | |
| 6 | | | |
| 7 | | | |
| 8 | | | |
| 9 | | | |
| 10 | | | |

**Appendix B2**   System summary

| System information | Comments |
|---|---|
| Computer | |
| Base memory | |
| Extended memory | |
| Expanded memory | |
| Video | |
| Network | |
| OS version | |
| Mouse | |
| Disk drives | |
| LPT ports (parallel) | |
| COM ports (serial) | |

**Appendix B3**    Rear panel connections

| Adaptor slot position | Function or application | Connector type |
| --- | --- | --- |
| 0 | | |
| 1 | | |
| 2 | | |
| 3 | | |
| 4 | | |
| 5 | | |
| 6 | | |
| 7 | | |

**Appendix B4**   Record of internal components

☐ Power supply

☐ System board

☐ Floppy disk drive(s)

☐ Hard disk drive(s)

☐ CD-ROM

☐ Expansion slots

☐ Video/graphics adaptor

☐ Disk drive adaptor and cables

☐ Serial and parallel port adaptors

☐ Loudspeaker

**Appendix B5**   System board component identification

| Component | Present | Circuit ref. number | Type |
|---|---|---|---|
| Power connectors | | | |
| Expansion slots | | Not applicable | |
| Keyboard socket | | Not applicable | |
| Speaker connector | | Not applicable | |
| Microprocessor/FPU | | | |
| Coprocessor | | | |
| ROM BIOS chip | | | |
| RAM | | | |
| Clock generator | | | |
| Crystal | | | |
| Integrated support chips | | | |
| Keyboard controller | | | |

**Appendix B6**   Evaluation of memory requirements

| Check made | Record |
|---|---|
| Microprocessor type | |
| Microprocessor speed | |
| Bus width | |
| Number of SIMM sockets | |
| Number of SIMMs installed | |
| Type of SIMMs | |
| Total memory capacity | |
| Memory requirements | |
| Additional memory needed | |
| Speed of memory needed | |

**Appendix B7**    System documentation

| Company reference: |
| --- |
| Manufacturer: |
| Model: |
| Serial number: |

| Microprocessor | Memory | BIOS |
| --- | --- | --- |
| Type: | Base: | Manufacturer: |
| Speed: | Ext:<br>Exp: | Type: |
| Cache: | Chips: | Date: |

| Drive | Manufacturer's data | Capacity | Interface | No. of heads | No. of cylinders | Sectors | WP comp | Partitions |
|-------|---------------------|----------|-----------|--------------|------------------|---------|---------|------------|
| C: | | | | | | | | |
| D: | | | | | | | | |

| Drive | Size | Capacity | Adaptor slot |
|-------|------|----------|--------------|
| A: | | | |
| B: | | | |

| Number | IRQ | Base address | Peripheral connected |
|--------|-----|--------------|----------------------|
| LPT1 | | | |
| LPT2 | | | |
| LPT3 | | | |

| Number | IRQ | Base address | Peripheral connected |
|--------|-----|--------------|----------------------|
| COM1   |     |              |                      |
| COM2   |     |              |                      |
| COM3   |     |              |                      |
| COM4   |     |              |                      |

| Slot | Type | IRQ | DMA | Base address | Comments |
|------|------|-----|-----|--------------|----------|
| 0    |      |     |     |              |          |
| 1    |      |     |     |              |          |
| 2    |      |     |     |              |          |
| 3    |      |     |     |              |          |
| 4    |      |     |     |              |          |
| 5    |      |     |     |              |          |
| 6    |      |     |     |              |          |
| 7    |      |     |     |              |          |

## AUTOEXEC.BAT

## CONFIG.SYS

## Appendix B8  Standard CMOS set-up display

```
                        Standard CMOS Setup


Date (m/d/y)       : Thur, Aug 01 1996    Base Memory      :
Time (h/m/s)       : 15:16:02             Ext.   Memory
                             Cyln   Head   WPCom   LZone   Sect   Size
Hard Disk C: Type  :
Hard Disk D: Type  :
Floppy Drive A     :
Floppy Drive B     :
Primary Display    :
Keyboard           :

ESC  : Exit        ↓→↑←  : Select
F2/F3 : Colour     PU/PD  : Modify
```

| Sun | Mon | Tues | Wed | Thu | Fri | Sat |
|-----|-----|------|-----|-----|-----|-----|
| 31  | 1   | 2    | 3   | 4   | 5   | 6   |
| 7   | 8   | 9    | 10  | 11  | 12  | 13  |
| 14  | 15  | 16   | 17  | 18  | 19  | 20  |
| 21  | 22  | 23   | 24  | 25  | 26  | 27  |
| 28  | 29  | 30   | 1   | 2   | 3   | 4   |

# Appendix C
## SIMM pinouts

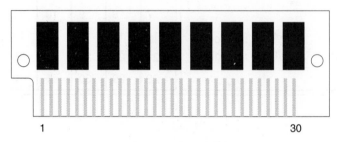

1                                          30

**C1**   30-pin SIMM

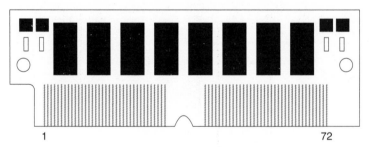

1                                          72

**C2**   72-pin SIMM

# Appendix D
## Adaptor slots

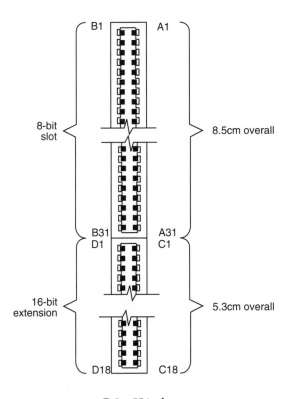

**D1** ISA slot

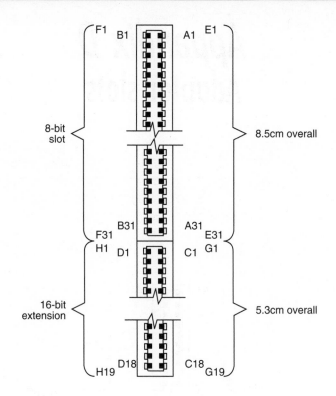

Rows A - D are upper (ISA) contacts

Rows E - H are lower (EISA) contacts

**D2**   EISA slot

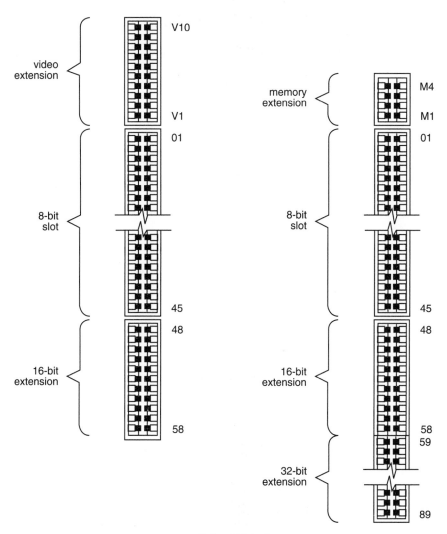

**D3**  MCA slot

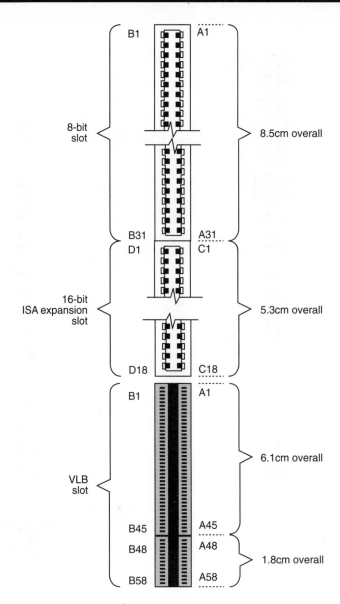

**D4**   VESA local bus slot

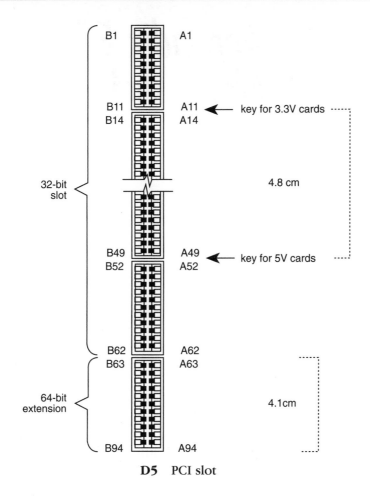

**D5** PCI slot

# Appendix E
## Adaptor cards

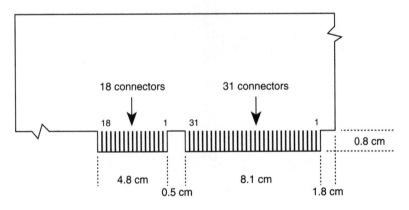

18 connectors

31 connectors

18   1   31   1

0.8 cm

4.8 cm

0.5 cm

8.1 cm

1.8 cm

**E1**  ISA adaptor

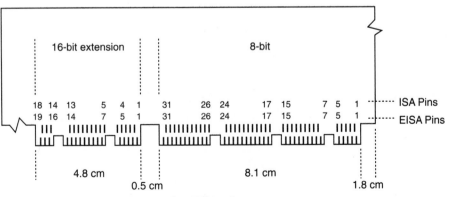

16-bit extension

8-bit

18 14 13   5   4   1   31   26 24   17 15   7 5   1 ······ ISA Pins
19 16 14   7   5   1   31   26 24   17 15   7 5   1 ······ EISA Pins

4.8 cm

0.5 cm

8.1 cm

1.8 cm

**E2**  EISA adaptor

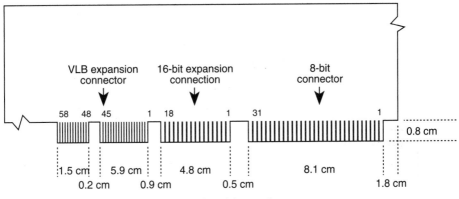

**E3** VESA local bus adaptor

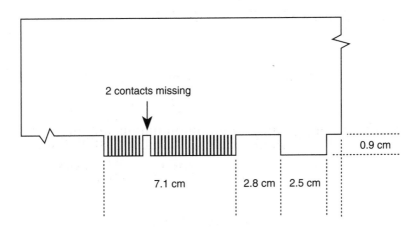

**E4** MCA adaptor

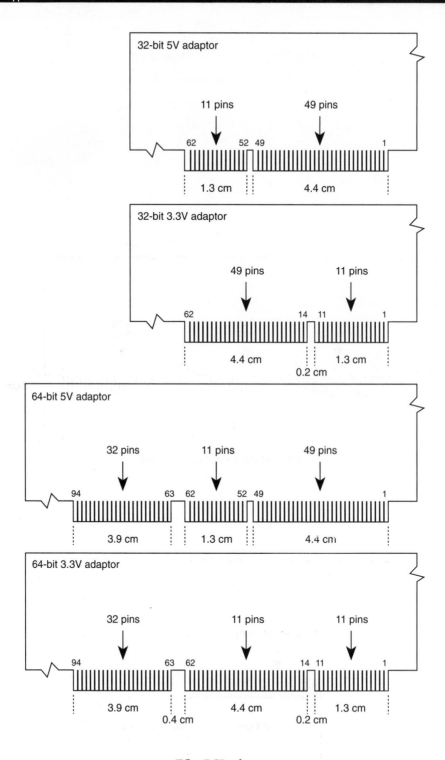

**E5**   PCI adaptor

# Appendix F
## Adaptor pin connections

(a)

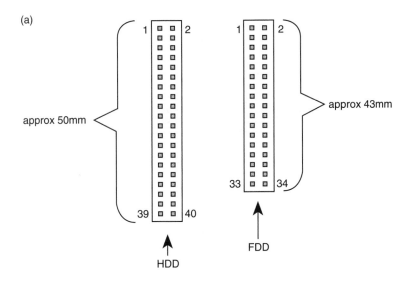

approx 50mm

approx 43mm

HDD

FDD

(b)

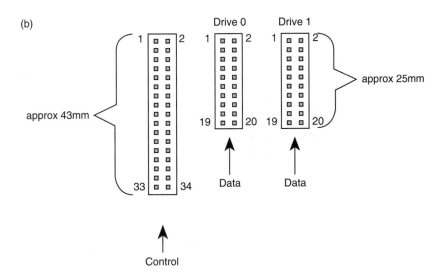

Drive 0    Drive 1

approx 43mm

approx 25mm

Data    Data

Control

**F1**   Adaptor card connectors: (a) IDE hard and floppy disk drives; (b) ST506 hard disk drive

Hard Disk Drive (HDD)

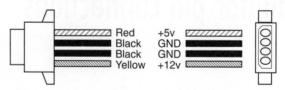

Floppy Disk Drive (FDD)

**F2    PSU to drive connectors**

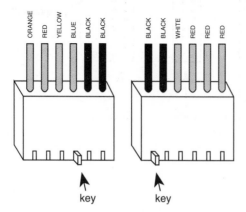

| | |
|---|---|
| Orange: | Power Good |
| Red: | +5V |
| Yellow: | +12V |
| Blue: | -12V |
| Black: | 0V |
| White: | -5V |

**F3    PSU to system board connectors**

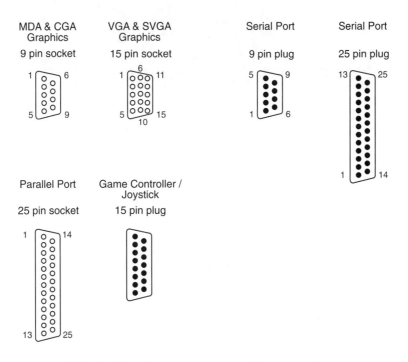

F4   Peripheral connectors on adaptor cards

# Appendix G
# Examples of POST error codes

The following tables provide a guide to some of the most popular types of POST error codes. It should be noted that some of the codes need the use of diagnostic tools and may not be seen if a failure occurs during operation. The symbol — indicates a long beep and • a short beep.

**G1**  Compaq

| Code | Error | Audible |
|------|-------|---------|
| 1xx  | System board (microprocessor) | — • |
| 2xx  | Memory | None |
| 3xx  | Keyboard | None |
| 4xx  | Parallel printer port | • • |
| 5xx  | Video display | • • — |
| 6xx  | Floppy disk drive | None or • • |
| 11xx | Comms (serial) port | • • |
| 17xx | Hard disk drive | • • or none |
| 24xx | VGA board | None |
| 86xx | Pointing device (mouse) | None |

## G2   IBM

| Code | Error |
|------|-------|
| 1xx | System board (microprocessor) |
| 2xx | Memory |
| 3xx | Keyboard |
| 4xx | Monochrome display |
| 5xx | Colour/graphics display |
| 6xx | Floppy disk drive/adaptor |
| 7xx | Math coprocessor |
| 9xx | Parallel printer adaptor |
| 10xx | Alternate printer adaptor |
| 11xx | Comms (serial) port |
| 12xx | Alternate comms port |
| 13xx | Game control adaptor |
| 14xx | Colour/graphics adaptor |
| 17xx | Hard disk drive |
| 24xx | VGA board |
| 86xx | Pointing device (mouse) |

# Appendix H
## Chipsets

The following tables provide just a few examples of the range of chipsets associated with microprocessor families and different bus systems. In some cases this can help in identifying the functions of particular chips, and they begin to lose their 'black box' unknown appearance. Each main support device is listed with the associated processor. The number indicates the type and is usually clearly displayed on the surface of the chip.

**H1**   Early 80286/80386 chipsets

| Function | 80286 | 80386 |
|---|---|---|
| Clock generator | 82284 | 82384 |
| Bus controller | 82288 | 82288 |
| Interrupt controller | 8259A | 8259A |
| DMA controller | 8089/82258 | 8237/82258 |
| Timer/counter | 8253/8254 | 8253/8254 |
| Math coprocessor | 80287 | 80287 |
| Keyboard controller | 8242 | 8242 |
| Integrated support | 82230/82231/82235 | 82230/82231/82235 |

**H2**   82340 chipset for 80386 systems

| Function | 80386SX | 80386DX |
|---|---|---|
| System controller | 82343 | 82346 |
| ISA bus controller | 82344 | 82344 |
| Data buffer | Internal 82343 | 82345 |
| Keyboard controller | 82C42 | 82C42 |

**H3**    Chipsets for use with PCI systems

| Function | | Comments |
| --- | --- | --- |
| PCI system controller | 82425EX | PCI, IDE, cache interfaces. Clocks and reset |
| ISA bridge | 82426EX | 2× DMA. 2× int. controllers. Timer/counter. ISA bus interface |
| Advanced integrated peripherals | 82091AA | FDD controller. 2× serial ports Dual IDE interface. Game port |
| PCMCIA/EIDE controller | 82092AA | Combines PCMCIA and LB for plug and play |
| System I/O–advanced programmable interrupt controller | 82379A | 2× int. controllers. Timer/counter. PCI-ISA bridge |
| Cache/memory subsystem | 82430 | PCI, cache, and memory controllers. Designed for Pentium |

# Glossary

*a.c.* Alternating current refers to a current that periodically reverses in direction several times per second. The domestic mains supply is alternating current and varies 50 times per second (50 Hz).

*Access time.* The time taken to write or read data from a storage device. Measured in fractions of a second: ms, millisecond (thousandth of a second); (μs, microsecond (millionth of a second); and ns, nanosecond (thousandth of a microsecond).

*Adaptor.* An electronic circuit board used to extend the system capabilities. Usually the card plugs into an expansion slot on the system board.

*Adaptor card.* See *Adaptor*.

*Address bus.* Bus used specifically for transferring address information.

*Address decoder.* Converts coded memory addresses into a format suitable for a chip to handle.

*Address strobe.* A signal used to indicate access to and produce data output from memory.

*Advanced set-up.* A menu within the CMOS set-up program that enables access to advanced configuration data.

*Arithmetic and logic unit (ALU).* The ALU undertakes the decision making by processing data and instructions.

*Backward compatiblility.* A term used to describe the compatibility of a system or device with older systems or devices.

*Base memory.* The first 640 Kb of memory. Also called conventional memory.

*Bit.* Used to describe a binary digit. It is the smallest unit of data in a digital system, having one of two values, 1 (on), or 0 (off). The term 'bit' will not be shortened when used as a unit of measurement.

*8-bit slot.* An adaptor slot that provides access to the 8-bit expansion bus.

*Block diagram.* A diagram that is used to give an outline of how a system works, using boxes to represent processes within the system.

*Burn-in.* The continued running of electronic equipment over a long period of time.

*Burst mode.* Burst mode of operation transfers data in a single burst without intervention from the microprocessor.

*Bus.* A collection of electrical connections or pathways, along which electrical signals move.

*Bus cycle pipelining.* Allows a second process cycle to start before the first has finished.

*Bus mastering.* A device that can take over the system bus from the microprocessor to control the flow of data.

*Byte.* A standard measure of memory and disk size, the byte consists of 8 bits of data. When used as a unit of measurement the term byte will be abbreviated to the lower-case letter 'b'.

*Cache.* A special type of very high speed RAM used to store data and instructions used regularly by the microprocessor.

*CD-ROM.* CD–read only memory. An optical storage medium similar to the audio compact disk (CD), used for permanent storage of data and programs. Although the information on an original pressing cannot be changed, it is now possible to obtain specialist equipment that enables the user to write to a CD-ROM.

*CGA display.* The colour graphics adaptor introduced colour to the world of PCs, allowing simple graphics as well as text.

*Chip.* Another term for *Integrated circuit*.

*Chip select.* A connection used to activate the chip.

*Chipset.* A collection of chips designed to work together in a PC with a particular microprocessor.

*Clock cycle.* The duration in which the clock pulse goes through a complete cycle of 'ON' and 'OFF'.

*Clocked logic.* A process of using timing pulses to step through instructions within a program.

*CMOS set-up.* See *Set-up*.

*Column address strobe (CAS).* An address strobe controlling columns.

*Compatible PC.* A system that is software compatible, but is significantly different in its hardware to the extent of not being able to use standard components freely.

*Continuity.* A continuous connection. Associated closely with resistance in terms of measuring the continuity of cables and fuses. Good continuity = low resistance; poor continuity = high resistance.

*Control bus.* Bus used specifically for transferring control signals.

*Conventional memory.* The first 640 Kb of memory. Also called base memory.

*Core frequency.* The internal operating frequency of a chip.

*CPU.* The central processing unit is also referred to as the processor or microprocessor and can be thought of as the 'brains' of the computer. It is discussed in more detail in Chapter 3.

*Crystal oscillator.* An electronic circuit producing a constant alternating signal. The 'crystal' is a small piece of quartz crystal housed in a metal can that is used to regulate the frequency of the oscillator.

*Current.* An electrical term used to describe the flow of electricity. Can be thought of as tiny particles flowing through a wire or circuit.

*Daisy chain.* The connection of several devices following one another to a cable.

*Data bus.* Bus used specifically for transferring data.

*d.c.* Direct current refers to current that, although it may vary, flows in one direction only. Batteries supply, and electronic circuits use direct current.

*Desktop PC.* For the purposes of this book the desktop PC will be considered to be that shown in Fig. 1.1(a) based on the original IBM AT design.

*DIP switch.* A small switch mounted on a circuit board usually used to select configuration settings in a similar way to a jumper.

*Diskette.* A magnetically coated disk used for the storage of data or programs. Also called a floppy disk, the diskette can be removed from the disk drive.

*Drive bay.* The slot where disk and CD-ROM drives are mounted.

*Execution unit.* A modern term used to describe an area of a chip that is designed to process data and instructions, e.g. the ALU.

*Expanded memory.* Physical memory above 1 Mb used in older systems, accessed as if it were conventional memory.

*Expansion bus.* An extension to the system bus that enables the expansion of the system using expansion or adaptor cards.

*Expansion card.* See *Adaptor card*.

*Expansion slot.* The connector that allows access to the expansion bus.

*Extended memory.* The memory area extending beyond 1 Mb.

*First-level (L1) cache.* Cache internal to the microprocessor used for specific tasks, e.g. data and instruction cache.

*Fixed disk drive.* Another term for a hard disk drive.

*Formatting.* A process of introducing magnetic tracks on to a floppy or hard disk.

*FRU.* A field replaceable unit is a module or component of the system that can be replaced relatively easily, and for economic reasons is normally not worth repairing as a unit, e.g. floppy disk drive.

*Hard disk drive.* A magnetic storage medium similar in purpose to the diskette, but with much greater capacity, and of a sealed-drive unit construction. The hard disk drive is not normally removable from the PC, but is designed as such in modern notebook and laptop systems.

*High memory area.* The first 64 Kb of extended memory.

*Integrated circuit.* An electronic circuit built on to a tiny, single piece of silicon material, encased in resin. The circuit can contain from a few components to several million, depending on the scale of integration.

*Jumper.* A two-pin connector used to join together pins to act as a switch. Jumpers are used to select configuration settings on system boards, drives and adaptors.

*Kilobyte.* Equivalent to 1024 bytes. (8 192 bits). The term Kilo should not be confused with the traditional meaning. In everyday use, kilo (k) refers to a multiple of 1000, but in computer terms the value for kilo (K) is 1024, e.g. 1 Kb = 1024 b = 8192 bits.

*Landing zone.* An inner cylinder on a hard disk drive at which the heads should be parked. This is achieved automatically on modern drives.

*Latch.* An electronic device that can be switched from one state to another, i.e. ON or OFF, 5 V or 0 V. Used in memory devices, the state of the latch can be used to represent cell content.

*LED.* A light emitting diode is an electronic indicator used in a similar way to an indicator bulb.

*Loop-back plug.* A pre-wired plug used in I/O sockets to simulate a peripheral device.

*Master.* The first of two installed hard disk drives.

*Megabyte.* Equivalent to 1024 kilobytes (1 048 576 bytes or 8 388 608 bits). In everyday use, mega refers to a multiple of 1 000 000, but in computer terms the value is 1 048 576, e.g. 1 Mb = 1024 Kb = 1 048 576 b = 8 388 608 bits. In real terms, 1 Mb can be approximated to the amount of space in memory, or on disk, that is needed to store about 1 000 000 characters.

*Megahertz (MHz).* Hertz is a unit of measurement of frequency (the number of times a signal changes per second). Megahertz represents a million changes per second.

*Memory.* An area consisting of electronic chips used to store data and instructions. Capacity is measured in bytes, Kb or Mb.

*Microprocessor.* In modern microcomputer systems using highly integrated components the CPU is referred to as the microprocessor. Often thought of as the 'brains' of a computer, the microprocessor temporarily stores and executes program instructions on data.

*Modem.* A peripheral device commonly used for connection to the telephone or similar network.

*Motherboard.* Another term used to describe the system board.

*Operating modes.* A term used to describe the different ways in which a microprocessor can function.

*Parity bit.* A single bit added to the data used to identify errors.

*Parity check.* An error-checking function used to identify when an error occurs in reading data.

*Partition.* A section on a hard disk drive configured as if it were a separate drive.

*Partitioning.* A process of dividing the physical structure of a hard disk drive into one or more logical drives.

*PC-clone.* A system that is both software and hardware compatible with the IBM AT standard. This means that a clone will operate software in the same way, and that hardware components are usually interchangeable. Care must be taken because although some components appear to be suitable, sometimes they are electrically incompatible and will not operate correctly.

*Port.* An inlet/outlet from the system used to connect peripheral devices, often via connectors on the rear panel. A parallel port transfers data several bits at once, whereas a serial port transfers one bit after another. Serial ports are therefore slower in operation. The parallel port is usually used for connection to a printer, and the serial port for a mouse or modem.

*Primary cache.* Cache memory contained within the microprocessor chip.

*Primary partition.* The main partition on a hard disk drive.

*RAM.* Random access memory. A specific type of memory used for temporary storage of data or instructions. It is continually written to and read from while the computer is operating.

*Read/write select.* A connection to a chip that indicates whether data are to be written or read.

*Reading.* The recovery of information from a storage device.

*'Ready' signal.* A signal used by a chip to indicate its readiness to transmit or receive data or instructions.

*Rectifier.* An electronic device that allows electric current to flow in one direction only. Used to convert a.c. into d.c.

*Refresh.* A process used to maintain the contents of dynamic RAM by topping up the charge on memory cells.

*Register.* An area within the microprocessor for temporary storage of data, address codes or operating instructions.

*Regulator.* An electronic device used to prevent unwanted variations in output voltage.

*'Reset' signal.* A signal used to 'restart' processes within a chip. An example includes the reset button on your PC which performs a soft-boot of the system.

*Resistance.* The opposition to the flow of electrical current. Measured in Ohms ($\Omega$). The lower the resistance, the more current flows. Cables and fuses should have low resistance along their length, just a few Ohms.

*Resolution.* A term used in video to describe the number of pixels, or dots, that can be displayed on a monitor screen. A high resolution results in a well-defined, clear image.

*Ribbon cable.* An electrical cable formed by combining several individual wires side-by-side to form the appearance of a ribbon.

*ROM.* Read only memory. A specific type of memory that under normal operation may be considered as permanent, i.e. cannot be altered by the user.

*Row address strobe (RAS).* An address strobe controlling rows.

*Scan code.* Keyboard scan code is a numerical code that identifies specific keys.

*Second-level (L2) cache.* Cache used for general-purpose functions. Originally external to the microprocessor but becoming more popular internally.

*Secondary cache.* Cache memory external to the microprocessor.

*Set-up.* The term set-up is made with reference to the CMOS set-up program, which can be accessed during the boot process. It enables modification of the CMOS settings for configuration information.

*Slave.* The second of two installed hard disk drives.

*Slot.* The connector into which adaptors are plugged, and which provides access to the expansion or system bus.

*Sound card.* An adaptor card used in multimedia systems to enhance the sound produced.

*Spike*. A mains spike is a large voltage pulse of very short duration caused by some form of interference in the mains supply.

*Standard set-up*. The main menu from the CMOS set-up program which enables modification of essential configuration data.

*Surface mount technology*. A manufacturing process used in the electronics industry that mounts electronic components such as chips directly on to the surface of the circuit board, i.e. not by inserting component leads through holes in the board.

*SVGA display*. The super virtual graphics array extends the number of modes used with standard VGA, providing even greater resolution.

*Switch mode power supply*. A special type of power supply used in modern domestic equipment that effectively operates by switching on and off several thousand times per second. The d.c. output voltage is controlled by the rate at which the supply switches.

*System board*. An electronic circuit board that forms the base for the main components of the system. Components are mounted either directly on to the board, or through the addition of plug-in expansion cards.

*System bus*. A term used to describe the data, address and control buses collectively.

*System speed*. A measure of the speed or frequency of the system clock that keeps the whole system in time. Sometimes referred to as clock speed, it is measured in MHz.

*Tape streamer*. Typically a high-quality, high-capacity tape recorder used to back-up the programs and files from a hard disk drive or other large storage device.

*Text display*. The original text displays used with monitors enabled text to be displayed on a different coloured background. Any form of graphics was text based and of poor quality.

*Transfer rate*. The rate at which data can be transferred. Measured in Kb/s or Mb/s, depending on the type of device.

*Transformer*. A device made from multiple windings of wire on a metal core, and used to convert an alternating voltage into an alternating voltage of different value.

*TTL digital electronics*. A type of electronics that uses only two specific levels of 0 V and 5 V to represent data as 'OFF' or 'ON'.

*Upper memory area*. The memory area from 640 Kb to 1 Mb.

*Upper memory blocks*. Small areas of the upper memory used to run device drivers and memory-resident programs.

*VGA display*. The virtual graphics array forms the basis of standards used today. It allows the use of 256 colours and offers much improved resolution, producing good-quality graphics.

*VLSI*. Very large scale integration is used to describe the level of integration of individual components, such as transistors, on to a single chip. VLSI refers to a technology that puts over 10 000 circuit components on to a single chip.

*Voltage*. An electrical term used to describe the driving force in an electrical circuit. Measured in volts, most people should be aware of the significant difference between the driving forces of the 240 V mains supply and a 6 V battery.

*Write-back caching*. A method by which data are transferred into cache without accessing memory.

*Write precompression*. A method of compensating for the smaller sectors towards the centre of a hard disk, improving data-write performance. This indicates the track at which write compensation begins.

*Write-through cache*. A method by which data are transferred to memory each time the processor writes to cache.

*Writing*. The saving of information to a storage device.

# Index